W9-BWY-034

Student Study Guide
to accompany

Early Childhood Education Today

Tenth Edition

George S. Morrison

Prepared by
Stefanie Kujaczynski
Marygrove College

PEARSON

Merrill
Prentice Hall

Upper Saddle River, New Jersey
Columbus, Ohio

Vice President and Executive Publisher: Jeffery W. Johnston
Publisher: Kevin M. Davis
Acquisitions Editor: Julie Peters
Editorial Assistant: Tiffany Bitzel
Senior Production Editor: Linda Hillis Bayma
Production Coordination: GGS Book Services
Design Coordinator: Diane C. Lorenzo
Cover Designer: Ali Mohrman
Cover Image: Corbis
Production Manager: Laura Messerly
Director of Marketing: David Gesell
Marketing Manager: Amy Judd
Marketing Coordinator: Brian Mounts

This book was printed and bound by Bind-Rite Graphics. The cover was printed by Phoenix Color Corp.

Pearson Prentice Hall™ is a trademark of Pearson Education, Inc.
Pearson® is a registered trademark of Pearson plc
Prentice Hall® is a registered trademark of Pearson Education, Inc.
Merrill® is a registered trademark of Pearson Education, Inc.

Pearson Education Ltd.
Pearson Education Singapore Pte. Ltd
Pearson Education Canada, Ltd.
Pearson Education—Japan

Pearson Education Australia Pty. Limited
Pearson Education North Asia Ltd.
Pearson Educatión de Mexico, S.A. de C.V.
Pearson Education Malaysia Pte. Ltd.

10 9 8 7 6 5 4 3 2 1
ISBN: 0-13-243436-9

Contents of the Student Study Guide

The *Student Study Guide* to accompany the tenth edition of *Early Childhood Education Today* by George Morrison is designed as a self-guided tool to assist you with the acquisition of text knowledge. The study guide will lead you through each chapter and assist you with identifying the important knowledge base for the early childhood professional. Each chapter contains the objectives, an overview, a study guide, making connections, and a self-check quiz.

I.   Chapter Objectives

The learner outcomes for each chapter are stated to help you identify the learning expectations for the chapter.

II.   Chapter Overview

Guiding questions are presented in the overview to help you focus on the most important issues in each chapter.

III. Study Guide

The study guide asks you to respond to questions that relate to the major topics of each chapter. Key terms found in the chapter are included in the study guide. Charts and boxes help you focus on the key concepts presented in the chapter.

IV.   Making Connections

Each chapter of the study guide contains an Internet connection to help enhance your knowledge about the major topics in the chapter. The Internet assignments will help you make connections between information in the chapter and the application of that information to practice. The assignments will support your development as an early childhood professional and assist you with the collection of information to support your future career.

V.   Self-Check

A sample quiz is included to provide you with an opportunity to check your knowledge of the content of each chapter. Questions on the quiz are similar in format to those provided in the Test Bank. Essay questions are included to guide your understanding of the material presented and to prepare you for your exams. Answers for the Self-Check are provided at the end of the *Student Study Guide*.

This guide is also available in Spanish.

Contents

Chapter 1   You and Early Childhood Education: What Does It Mean to Be a Professional?   1

Chapter 2   Early Childhood Education Today: Public Policy and Current Issues   15

Chapter 3   Observing and Assessing Young Children: Effective Teaching Through Appropriate Evaluation   24

Chapter 4   The Past and the Present: Prologue to the Future   35

Chapter 5   Theories Applied to Teaching and Learning: Foundations for Practice   45

Chapter 6   Early Childhood Programs: Applying Theories to Practice   58

Chapter 7   Child Care: Meeting the Needs of Children, Parents, and Families   73

Chapter 8   The Federal Government: Supporting Children's Success   81

Chapter 9   Infants and Toddlers: Foundation Years for Learning   92

Chapter 10   The Preschool Years: Getting Ready for School and Life   111

Chapter 11   Kindergarten Education: Learning All You Need to Know   131

Chapter 12   The Primary Grades: Preparation for Lifelong Success   148

Chapter 13   Technology and Young Children: Education for the Information Age   161

Chapter 14   Guiding Children: Helping Children Become Responsible   173

Chapter 15   Multiculturalism: Education for Living in a Diverse Society   190

Chapter 16   Children with Special Needs: Appropriate Education for All   205

Chapter 17   Parent, Family, and Community Involvement: Cooperation and Collaboration   220

Self-Check Answer Key by Chapter   233

CHAPTER 1

YOU AND EARLY CHILDHOOD EDUCATION: WHAT DOES IT MEAN TO BE A PROFESSIONAL?

I.   **Chapter Objectives**

Learner outcomes

The learner will
- Describe the early childhood professional
- Explain the roles of the early childhood professional
- Define the terminology of early childhood education
- Describe the hierarchy of the early childhood profession

II.   **Chapter Overview**

Who is an early childhood professional?

What can you do to demonstrate the personal, educational, professional practice, and public dimensions of professionalism?

How can you prepare for a career in early childhood education?

What does the future hold for you as an early childhood professional?

III.   Chapter 1 Study Guide

Directions: As you read the chapter, answer the following questions. Use the guide to study the chapter information.

The Early Childhood Professional

1.   Define the term *early childhood professional.*

_____

_____

_____

The Four Dimensions of Professionalism

2.   Identify and explain the components of the four dimensions of a high-quality early childhood professional.

Professional Characteristics
Character Traits

Emotional Qualities

Physical Health

Mental Health

Educational Attainment
Degree programs (List the related professional positions referred to in Figure 1.2)

Child Development Association (CDA) National Credentialing Program (List the related professional positions referred to in Figure 1.2)

Child Development Association Professional Preparation Program (List the related professional positions referred to in Figure 1.2)

Professional Practice
Know Children and How They Develop

Develop a Philosophy of Education

Plan

Assess

Report

Reflect and Think

Teach

Collaborate with Parents, Families, and Community Partners

Engage in Ethical Practice

Seek Ongoing Professional Development

Public Presentation
Advocacy

Communicate with Others

Represent the Profession

3.   A philosophy of education is a set of beliefs about how children develop and learn, and what and how they should be taught (see text pages 12–14). When responding to the following questions consider all children from birth through age eight.

Write your beliefs about children and learning.

_____

_____

_____

_____

_____

_____

_____

_____

_____

_____

I believe the purposes of early childhood education are…

_____

_____

_____

_____

I believe that children learn best when…

_____

_____

_____

_____

The curriculum of any classroom should include certain "basics" that contribute to a child's social, emotional, intellectual, and physical development. These basics are…

_____

_____

_____

_____

Children learn best in an environment that promotes learning. Features of a good learning environment are…

_____

_____

_____

_____

All children have certain needs that must be met if they are to grow and learn at their best. Some of these basic needs are…

_____

_____

_____

_____

I would meet these needs by…

_____

_____

_____

_____

A teacher should have certain qualities and behave in certain ways. Qualities I think are important for teaching include…

_____

_____

_____

_____

Now rewrite your belief statements to create your first draft of your philosophy of early childhood education. Continue to revisit this statement as you grow and develop as an early childhood professional.

4.   Define the term *developmentally appropriate practice* (see text page 12).

_____

_____

_____

How Can You Prepare for a Career in Early Childhood Education?

5.   **Refer to Figure 1.4 in the text, "Assessing Your Professional Development."** Identify four or more things you will do this term to help prepare yourself for a career in early childhood education. List the four items you selected and describe your plan to accomplish your goals.

_____

_____

_____

_____

_____

_____

_____

6. Refer to the Diversity Tie-In "Multiculturalism and Professionalism" to answer the following:

How does knowledge of diversity support professionalism?

How does knowledge of diversity allow you to better support the growth and development of all children?

How does knowledge of diversity allow you to make better judgments regarding curriculum, assessment, environment, etc.?

_____

_____

_____

What Does the Future Hold for the Early Childhood Professional?

7. List the changing conditions of the future that will influence you and the profession in the future. Note key facts about each condition.

Future Influences on the Early Childhood Profession

a.	b.
c.	d.
e.	f.
g.	h.

Rediscovering the Role of Today's Early Childhood Professional

8. The role of the early childhood professional today is very different from what it was two or three years ago. The dimensions of professionalism and the characteristics of a high-quality professional remain the same; responsibilities, expectations, and roles have changed. Explain the roles listed below and how they are changing or being redefined.

Teacher as an instructional leader.

_____

_____

_____

Intentional teaching of state, district, and program goals and standards.

_____

_____

_____

Performance-based accountability for learning.

_____

_____

_____

Teaching of literacy and reading.

_____

_____

_____

Increased emphasis on assessing what children learn and using the results of assessment to plan for teaching and learning.

_____

_____

_____

_____   •

_____

A new meaning of child-centered education.

_____

_____

_____

_____

IV. **Making Connections**

Explore the National Association for the Education of Young Children (NAEYC) web site. Using the Internet Log list the (URL) location and describe at least five things on the site that will help you become an early childhood professional. Consider your areas of focus for question 5 on page 7 of this guide.

National Association for the Education of Young Children
http://www.naeyc.org

Internet Log

Use this log to keep a record of the web sites that have information for the early childhood professional. Update your log each time you locate new information that is useful to you as you become an early childhood professional.

V.   Chapter 1 Self-Check

Multiple Choice Questions Select the best answer.

1.   An early childhood professional works with children from_____.
       Hint: **See "What Is a Professional?"**
       A.   Age four to age eight.
       B.   Birth to age eight.
       C.   Birth to age six.
       D.   Preschool through second grade.

2.   Which of the following is not one of the dimensions of a high-quality professional?
       Hint: **See "The Four Dimensions of Professionalism."**
       A.   Personal characteristics
       B.   Educational degree
       C.   Professional practice
       D.   Public presentation

3.   Which of the following is the most essential emotional quality for an early childhood professional?
       Hint: **See "Emotional Qualities."**
       A.   Caring
       B.   Empathy
       C.   Compassion
       D.   Kindness

4.   Early childhood professionals must be able to _____.
       Hint: **See "Professional Practice."**
       A.   Assess learning.
       B.   Collaborate with colleagues and families.
       C.   Seek continued professional development.
       D.   All of the above.

5.   Candidates for the Child Development Associate credential must demonstrate their ability to provide competent care and early education practice by meeting which of the following CDA goals?
       Hint: **See Table 1.1, "CDA Competency Goals and Functional Areas."**
       A.   To establish and maintain a safe and healthy learning environment
       B.   To earn a degree
       C.   To observe and assess children's development
       D.   To advocate for children and families

6. The professional practice dimension of professionalism does <u>not</u> include which of the following?
    ***Hint*: See "Professional Practice."**
    A. Knowledge of DAP and DCAP
    B. Knowledge of planning, assessing, reporting, reflecting, and thinking
    C. Knowledge of ethical practice and ethical conduct
    D. Knowledge of credentialing programs

7. A *philosophy of education* is_____.
    ***Hint*: See "Professional Practice."**
    A. A set of beliefs about how children learn, develop, and what and how they should be taught.
    B. A set of objectives and goals for instructional delivery.
    C. A set of beliefs about how children learn.
    D. A description of methodology for content delivery.

8. Planning is an essential part of practicing the art and craft of teaching. Which of the following is not a true statement about planning?
    ***Hint*: See "Professional Practice."**
    A. The teacher sets the goals for the children.
    B. The planning process takes place periodically.
    C. The teacher selects activities to help children achieve planning goals.
    D. Effective teachers plan and collaborate with others.

9. Advocacy is defined in many ways and includes many activities. *Advocacy* is defined in the text as_____.
    ***Hint*: See "Public Presentation."**
    A. The process of lobbying lawmakers to secure services for children and families.
    B. The act of promoting the causes of children and families to the profession and the public.
    C. The act of communicating with community leaders to enlist the support for children and families.
    D. The act of working with authorities to speak on behalf of children in crisis.

10. A_____ refers to all who work with, care for, and teach children between birth and age eight.
    ***Hint*: See "What Is a Professional?"**
    A. Teacher
    B. Professional
    C. Caregiver
    D. Educator

11. *Ethical conduct* is the exercise of responsible behavior with children, families, colleagues, and community members. Ethical practice is a component of which of the following dimensions?
    Hint: See **"Engaging in Ethical Practice."**
    A. Personal characteristics
    B. Educational attainment
    C. Professional practice
    D. Public presentation

12. Diversity training and education is designed to provide additional information to early educators to allow them to better meet the needs of children. Which statement below is not true of diversity education for professionals?
    Hint: See **"Why Are There Diversity Tie-Ins?"**
    A. Allows you to make curricular modifications and desensitize controversial issues.
    B. Enables you to teach students regardless of their cultural, ethnic, or socioeconomic status.
    C. Helps you apply multicultural knowledge and information in your teaching.
    D. Provides you with learning ideas that support children's growth and development regardless of culture background, socioeconomic status, or gender.

Discussion Questions

1. Early childhood professionals work with children and families every day. The early childhood professional must know about and demonstrate essential knowledge of the profession and professional practice. According to the text, what is included in this essential knowledge?

2. Advocacy is one responsibility of the early childhood professional. Discuss the relationship of advocacy and the National Association for the Education of Young Children (NAEYC) Code of Ethical Conduct located in Appendix A of your textbook and also described in Chapter 1, as they relate to the early childhood profession.

3. Identify and discuss the elements of professional practice as they influence the development of your philosophy of education.

CHAPTER 2

**EARLY CHILDHOOD EDUCATION TODAY: PUBLIC POLICY
AND CURRENT ISSUES**

I.   **Chapter Objectives**

Learner outcomes

The learner will
- Describe the critical issues facing children and families today
- Explain how social, political, economic, and educational issues influence and change child rearing, early childhood education, and teaching
- Explore the implications contemporary issues have for curriculum, teaching, and life outcomes of children and families
- Explore how childhood programs and professionals help solve contemporary social problems

II.   **Chapter Overview**

How are public policy and current issues changing early childhood education?

How do social, political, economic, and educational issues influence and change child rearing, early childhood education, and teaching?

What are some implications that contemporary issues have for curriculum, teaching, and the life outcomes of children and families?

How can early childhood programs and teachers help solve contemporary social problems?

III.   Chapter 2 Study Guide

Directions: As you read the chapter, answer the following questions. Use the guide to study the chapter information.

Public Policy and Current Issues

1.   What is public policy? How do public policies impact young children, families, and professionals working in the field of early childhood education?

_____

_____

_____

_____

_____

2.   Public policy affects the care and education of young children and frequently creates public issues. Children and families are confronted with many issues that increase risk factors related to their education and life outcomes. Issues confronting children and families are in the news daily. Read the headlines in Figure 2.1. Observe your local newspaper(s) for headlines that highlight young children and their families. List below the information you find in those local sources.

_____

_____

_____

_____

_____

_____

_____

_____

3.	Identify the ways that families are changing.

Structure	Roles	Responsibilities

4.	Early childhood professionals agree that the best way to meet the needs of children and families is through their families. Identify the four reasons given for working with children through their family unit.

a.
b.
c.
d.

5.	Many contemporary issues affect families and early childhood professionals. As you review the topics below, refer to the statistical tables and figures in the text to assist your understanding of the issues and how they affect children, families, and early childhood professionals today.

	Children	Families	EC Professionals
Working Parents			
Affluent Parents			

Fathers			
Single Parents			
Teenage Parents			

6.   Poverty has serious negative consequences for children and families. More than four million children under the age of six live in poverty. Discuss the ways poverty is detrimental to students' achievement and life prospects.

_____

_____

_____

_____

_____

7.   Identify the leading children's illnesses discussed in the text and what early childhood professionals can do to help with the problems associated with childhood illness.

_____

_____

_____

_____

_____

_____

_____

_____

8. Public interest in brain research has increased over the last several years. Identify the key findings of this research as it relates to the care and education of young children.

_____

_____

_____

_____

_____

_____

_____

_____

9. Explain how the federal and state governments have become involved in early childhood programs.

_____

_____

_____

_____

_____

10. Discuss the relationship between preschools and public schools. How has this relationship changed?

_____

_____

_____

_____

_____

11.   Summarize the reasons parents lobby for public support of early childhood programs.

_____

_____

_____

_____

_____

_____

_____

_____

IV.   <u>Making Connections</u>

Find out who your U.S. and state senators and representatives are and how to contact them.

Learn how your representatives vote on legislation that supports quality early childhood care for all children. Visit the **Children's Defense Fund** web site (www.childrensdefense.org) and find out how to write/call/visit/email your representatives.

	U.S. Senator	U.S. Representative
Name: Contact Information:		
Name: Contact Information:		

V.   Chapter 2 Self-Check

Multiple Choice Questions Select the best answer.

1.   Which of the following is <u>not</u> one of the contemporary social issues affecting decisions that families and early childhood professionals must make about the education and care of young children?
   Hint: **See "Hot Topics in Early Childhood Education."**
   A.   Problems of child abuse
   B.   Large number of children and families who live in poverty
   C.   Low-quality care and education of young children
   D.   All of the above are issues affecting families and early childhood professionals

2.   Families are in a continual state of change as a result of social issues and changing times. Which of the following is <u>not</u> true of families in the twenty-first century?
   Hint: **See "Family Issues."**
   A.   Structure; families now include arrangements other than the traditional nuclear family.
   B.   Numbers; families now include more children than ever before.
   C.   Roles; as families change so do the roles that parents and other family members perform.
   D.   Responsibilities; as families change, many parents are not able to provide or cannot afford to pay for adequate and necessary care for their children.

3.   Programs that provide education and support for literacy, health care, nutrition, healthy living, abuse prevention, obesity prevention, and parenting are examples of:
   Hint: **See "Family Issues."**
   A.   The family-centered approach to meeting the needs of children and families.
   B.   The family approach to meeting the needs of children and families.
   C.   The child care approach to meeting the needs of children and families.
   D.   The partnership approach to meeting the needs of children and families.

4.   The role of the father and his involvement in child rearing is highly researched today. Which of the following is true about fathers today?
   Hint: **See "Fathers Rediscovered."**
   A.   Fathers are rarely granted custody of their children.
   B.   Fathers of today are more involved in parenting and child rearing.
   C.   The early childhood profession does little to include or educate fathers regarding best practices of child rearing.
   D.   Fathers still remain in the role of passive parent.

5.   Children living in poverty are more likely to be _____.
     Hint: See "Poverty."
     A.   Retained in school.
     B.   More "highly engaged" than others in school.
     C.   More likely to have a learning disability.
     D.   From families who are unable to assist them with homework.

6.   Brain research and other studies are influencing our ideas about how children learn, how to teach them, and what they should learn. Which of the following is <u>not</u> a conclusion about young children based on this research?
     Hint: See **"Brain Research and Early Childhood Education."**
     A.   Human development is based on dynamic and continuous interaction between biology and experience.
     B.   Evidence supports that children are born with fixed intelligences.
     C.   Human relationships are the building blocks of healthy development.
     D.   Children are active participants in their own development.

7.   Increasing acts of violence lead to proposals for how to provide violence-free homes and educational environments for children. Which of the following is <u>not</u> a proposal to help curb violence?
     Hint: See **"Stress and Violence."**
     A.   Using the V-chip
     B.   Teach children to get along with their peers without the use of violence
     C.   Programs that prevent and curb bullying
     D.   Limiting the exposure of toys that encourage violent behavior

8.   The states and the federal government are exerting more control over education. One of the dramatic changes occurring in society today is the expanded role of the federal government in the reform of public education. Which of the following is <u>not</u> one of the ways the federal government is exerting more control over education?
     Hint: See **"Federal Support for Reform."**
     A.   Reform of education funding to take away state control of education.
     B.   Reform of Head Start by making it more academic, emphasizing early literacy skills.
     C.   Reform of education so that all children will be able to read on grade level.
     D.   Reform of education to close the achievement gap.

9.   The most common chronic childhood illness in the United States is_____.
     Hint: See **"Wellness and Healthy Living."**
     A.   Obesity.
     B.   Asthma.
     C.   Lead poisoning.
     D.   Chicken pox.

10. A current trend in federal funding for early childhood programs is to consolidate monies into block grants. A *block grant* is_____.
    ***Hint*: See "Government Involvement in Early Childhood Programs."**
    A. Federal funding given directly to states for specific programs.
    B. Federal money given to states to provide services according to broad general guidelines.
    C. Federal money given to states that is controlled by the federal government, giving the state no say in the way the money is spent.
    D. Sums of money given to states to start new early childhood programs.

11. Early childhood professionals must not take for granted the environments that children are raised in. Which of the following does <u>not</u> affect the growth and development of young children?
    ***Hint*: See "Social Issues."**
    A. Many children live in a home which has at least one person who smokes.
    B. Many children live in substandard housing with unhealthy conditions.
    C. Many children live in overcrowded conditions.
    D. Many children live in a home with one or more pets.

12. Millions of children are reared in single-parent households, which has many implications for early childhood professionals. Which of the following is <u>not</u> a true statement?
    ***Hint*: See "Changing Family Units."**
    A. Single parents rarely have unique needs or requests of early childhood professionals.
    B. Early childhood programs are developing curricula to support children and their single parents.
    C. Early childhood professionals conduct parenting seminars.
    D. Single parents often seek expert advice from early childhood professionals.

Discussion Questions

1. Explain the four reasons the family systems approach is advocated for meeting the needs of children and families.

2. Explain why parents lobby for public support of early childhood education.

3. Discuss the hot topics in early childhood education today.

CHAPTER 3

OBSERVING AND ASSESSING YOUNG CHILDREN: EFFECTIVE TEACHING THROUGH APPROPRIATE EVALUATION

I.   **Chapter Objectives**

Learner outcomes

The learner will
- Understand the importance of appropriate and accurate assessment
- Develop an understanding of the purposes and uses of assessment
- Describe the purpose of observation as an assessment tool
- Identify a variety of ways to assess children's development, learning, and behavior

II.   **Chapter Overview**

What is assessment, and why is it important?

Why is it important for you to know how to assess?

What are the purposes and uses of assessment and observation?

What are some major ways to assess children's development, learning, and behavior?

What issues are involved in assessment?

III.   Chapter 3 Study Guide

Directions: As you read the chapter, answer the following questions. Use the guide to study the chapter information.

What Is Assessment?

1.   Define *assessment.*

_____

_____

_____

_____

_____

2.   What is appropriate assessment?

_____

_____

_____

_____

_____

3.   Identify the purposes of assessment for each of the following groups:

Children	Families	Early Childhood Professionals	Early Childhood Programs	The Public

4.   Define *high-stakes assessment.*

_____

_____

_____

Examples of high-stakes assessment:

a. _____

b. _____

5.   Define *authentic assessment.*

_____

_____

_____

6.   What are the characteristics of authentic assessment?

a. _____

b. _____

c. _____

d. _____

e. _____

f. _____

g. _____

h. _____

i. _____

7.	Fill in each section to define portfolio assessment.

What is portfolio assessment?	What items are included in a portfolio?	How is portfolio assessment used?

Assessment for School Readiness

8.	A comprehensive screening program for children who will enter kindergarten in the fall includes:

a. _____

b. _____

c. _____

d. _____

9.	What is the purpose of screening children before they enter kindergarten?

_____

_____

_____

_____

_____

_____

_____

10. Listed below are various screening instruments and observational recording techniques listed in the text. Identify the type of instrument (screening, observation), the recommended age, and the information gained from the assessment instrument.

Screening Instruments and Observation Records

Instrument	Type	Age	Assessment Information
BRIGANCE® Preschool Screen II			
High/Scope Child Observation Record			
DIAL-3			

What Is Observation?

11. _____ is the intentional, _____ act of looking at the

_____ of a child in a particular setting, program, or situation.

12. What is "kidwatching"?

_____

_____

_____

13. What are the purposes of observation?

_____

_____

_____

_____

_____

_____

_____

_____

_____

14.   Review the process for conducting observations. Complete the chart below.

Step 1: _____
Step 2: _____
Step 3: _____
Step 4: _____

15.   Reporting to parents is an important responsibility of the early childhood professional.
       Identify the guidelines for reporting assessment information to parents:

       a. _____

       _____

b. _____

_____

_____

c. _____

_____

_____

d. _____

_____

_____

e. _____

_____

_____

What Are the Critical Assessment Issues?

16.   Explain the following assessment issues and describe the implications for early childhood professionals.

Assessment and Accountability _____

_____

_____

_____

High-Stakes Testing _____

_____

_____

_____

Test Bias _____

_____

_____

_____

How young is too young? _____

_____

_____

_____

IV.   Making Connections

Go to the ERIC web site below to read Lillian Katz's article on developmentally appropriate assessment. Compare the information in the article with the information found in Figure 3.2 and Table 3.1.   List your findings. Be prepared to share your findings in class.

A Developmental Approach to Assessment of Young Children
http://ceep.crc.uiuc.edu/eecearchive/digests/1997/katz97.pdf

V.   Chapter 3 Self-Check

Multiple Choice Questions Select the best answer.

1.   Assessment occurs through which of the following:
       Hint: See "What Is Assessment?"
       A.   Observation, teacher opinion, tests.
       B.   Teacher opinion, parent interviews, tests.
       C.   Observation, tests, examination of student products.
       D.   Observation, parent interviews, examination of student products.

2.   Which of the following is not a true statement regarding authentic assessment?
       Hint: See "Authentic Assessment."
       A.   A paper and pencil test designed by the teacher to test what has been taught in a lesson.
       B.   Assesses children on the basis of their actual work.
       C.   Provides for ongoing assessment over the entire school year.
       D.   Makes assessment part of the learning process.

3. The _____ is used by teachers or other observers to assess young children's development by observing their typical classroom activities.
    Hint: **See "Assessment for School Readiness."**
    A. BRIGANCE® Preschool Screen II.
    B. DIAL-3.
    C. High/Scope Child Observation Record.
    D. Portfolios.

4. The _____ is an instrument designed for screening large numbers of prekindergarten children on the development of motor skills, concepts, and language skills.
    Hint: **See "Assessment for School Readiness."**
    A. BRIGANCE® Preschool Screen II.
    B. DIAL-3.
    C. High/Scope Child Observation Record.
    D. Portfolios.

5. The _____ is an evaluation instrument designed to evaluate skills, behaviors, and concepts such as color recognition.
    Hint: **See "Assessment for School Readiness."**
    A. BRIGANCE® Preschool Screen II.
    B. DIAL-3.
    C. High/Scope Child Observation Record.
    D. Portfolios.

6. Observations are designed to gather information on which to base decisions, make recommendations, develop curriculum, and plan activities and learning strategies. The purposes of observations include which of the following?
    Hint: **See "What Is Observation?"**
    A. To determine the cognitive, linguistic, social, emotional, and physical development of children.
    B. To identify children's interests and learning styles.
    C. To provide information to parents.
    D. All of the above.

7. Today there is tremendous emphasis on testing and the use of tests to measure achievement. The emphasis will continue for all of the following reasons <u>except</u>:
    Hint: **See "What Are Critical Assessment Issues?"**
    A. The public sees assessment as a means of making schools and teachers accountable for teaching the nation's children.
    B. Assessment is seen as playing a critical role in improving education.
    C. Assessment results can be used to structure curriculum and instructional practices.
    D. Professionals view testing as an important way to gather individual student outcomes to report to parents.

8.	Some states are currently tying teacher salaries to student achievement. This process is referred to as performance-based pay. Which of the following statements defines performance-based pay?
	***Hint*: See "What Are Critical Assessment Issues?"**
	A.	Performance-based pay is given to teachers as stipend for the development of authentic assessment tools used for young children.
	B.	Performance-based pay is given in the form of a paid bonus when children meet specific achievement goals.
	C.	Performance-based pay is given to teachers who review and receive training in a variety of assessment tools and techniques.
	D.	Performance-based pay is given when teachers follow a developmentally appropriate approach to assessment.

9.	Test bias refers to:
	***Hint*: See "What Are Critical Assessment Issues?"**
	A.	A teacher's attitude about a specific assessment tool.
	B.	Items on a test that give certain groups of students an advantage.
	C.	Items on a test that put certain groups of students at an unfair advantage.
	D.	The items on a test that are easily answered by all groups of students.

10.	The federal government is in the process of testing all children who participate in Head Start to determine if they have achieved the knowledge and skills specified in the Head Start Performance Standards. According to the text, some early childhood professionals believe that:
	***Hint*: See "What Are Critical Assessment Issues?"**
	A.	Testing is appropriate for children of all ages.
	B.	Testing should begin when children enter an early care and education program to ensure program accountability.
	C.	Assessment should not be used in early care and education programs.
	D.	Four- and five-year-old children are too young to be subjected to such testing.

11.	Appropriate assessment strategies can help the early childhood professional find solutions to which of the following problems?
	***Hint*: See "What Is Assessment?"**
	A.	How to modify instruction, how individual children are progressing, and what information can be reported about specific developmental domains.
	B.	How to modify instruction, how much individual assistance is required, and what information can be reported about specific developmental domains.
	C.	How successful homework has been, how individual children are progressing, and what information can be reported about specific developmental domains.
	D.	How to modify instruction, how individual children are progressing, and what classroom materials are the most beneficial.

12. Reliable assessment is a central part of all early childhood programs. Which of the following is <u>not</u> an indicator of effective assessment strategies for early childhood programs?

    ***Hint*: See "Assessment of Young Children."**

    A.   Ethical principles guide all assessment practices.
    B.   What is assessed is developmentally and educationally appropriate.
    C.   Decisions about children are made on the basis of a single assessment.
    D.   Staff and families are knowledgeable about assessment.

Discussion Questions

1.   Identify and explain the steps involved in the process of systemic, purposeful observation.

2.   Explain how the early childhood professional reports assessment information to parents.

3.   Discuss the use of portfolios as an assessment tool. What, if any, are the problems with the use of portfolio assessment?

CHAPTER 4

THE PAST AND THE PRESENT: PROLOGUE TO THE FUTURE

I. **Chapter Objectives**

Learner outcomes

The learner will
- Explain the importance of the theories of great educators
- Describe the beliefs of Luther, Comenius, Locke, Rousseau, Pestalozzi, Owen, Froebel, Dewey, Maslow, Erickson, and Gardner
- Examine the influence of great educators' beliefs on early childhood programs today
- Assess the influence of historical events on people, agencies, and legislation
- Discuss the influence of the past of early childhood education on the future direction of early childhood education

II. **Chapter Overview**

Why is it important for you to have an appreciation for the ideas, professional accomplishments, and contributions of great educators?

What are the basic beliefs of people who have influenced early childhood education: Luther, Comenius, Locke, Rousseau, Pestalozzi, Owen, Froebel, Dewey, Maslow, Erickson, and Gardner?

How have the beliefs and ideas of great educators such as Piaget and Vygotsky influenced early childhood programs?

How is contemporary education influenced by historical people and events?

III. Chapter 4 Study Guide

Directions: As you read the chapter, answer the following questions. Use the guide to study the chapter information.

Why Is the Past Important?

1. List and explain the five reasons why knowing about the past is important for you as an early childhood educator:

a.
b.
c.
d.
e.

Historical Figures and Their Influence on Early Childhood Education

2.   Complete the table below indicating each notable educator's contributions to early childhood education.

Historical Figures and Their Influence on Early Childhood Education

Educator	Contributions
Martin Luther	
John Amos Comenius	
John Locke	
Jean-Jacques Rousseau	
Johann Heinrich Pestalozzi	
Robert Owen	
Friedrich Wilhelm Froebel	
Maria Montessori	
Margarethe Schurz	

Elizabeth Peabody
Susan Blow
Patty Smith Hill
John Dewey
Jean Piaget
Lev Vygotsky
Abraham Maslow
Erik Erikson
Howard Gardner

From Luther to the Present: The Essentials of Good Educational Practices

3.   What are the essential concepts necessary for good educational practice as they relate to all children?

_____

_____

_____

_____

_____

_____

_____

_____

_____

4.   What are the basic concepts essential to good educational practices as they relate to all teachers?

a. _____

b. _____

c. _____

d. _____

e. _____

f. _____

g. _____

h. _____

i. _____

j. _____

k. _____

5.   What are the basic concepts essential to good educational practice as they relate to families?

_____

_____

_____

_____

_____

_____

_____

Views of Children Through the Ages

6.   Explain each of the following views of children.

Miniature Adults_____

_____

_____

_____

Sinful Children _____

_____

_____

_____

Blank Tablets _____

_____

_____

_____

Growing Plants _____

_____

_____

_____

Property _____

_____

_____

_____

Investments in the Future _____

_____

_____

_____

Persons with Rights _____

_____

_____

_____

7. The High/Scope Perry Preschool program is frequently cited to demonstrate how high-quality preschool programs provide a higher return for dollars spent. List the three monetary returns identified in your text:

a. _____

b. _____

c. _____

Child-Centered Education

8.   Define *child-centered education* and list the guiding principles.

_____

_____

_____

_____

_____

_____

_____

_____

IV.   Making Connections

Select one of the great educators from the past. Conduct an Internet search to learn more about your selection. Attempt to identify unique characteristics or aspects of your educator's theory or expertise not previously mentioned in the text. Record your findings on your Internet log begun in Chapter 1 of this study guide.

Be prepared to report your findings in class.

V.   Chapter 4 Self-Check

Multiple Choice Questions Select the best answer.

1.   The first educator to develop a planned, systemic program for educating young children was_____.
       Hint: See **"Historical Figures and Their Influence on Early Childhood Education."**
       A.   Friedrich Froebel.
       B.   Maria Montessori.
       C.   John Dewey.
       D.   Abraham Maslow.

2.   Martin Luther emphasized the necessity of establishing schools to teach children to:
       Hint: See **"Historical Figures and Their Influence on Early Childhood Education."**
       A.   Read
       B.   Read and write Latin
       C.   Speak Latin
       D.   Solve mathematical problems

3.   *Orbis Pictus,* the first picture book for children, was written by:
     Hint: See "Historical Figures and Their Influence on Early Childhood Education."
     A.   John Locke
     B.   Robert Owen
     C.   John Amos Comenius
     D.   Martin Luther

4.   _____'s theory of education is usually referred to as *progressivism.*
     Hint: See "Historical Figures and Their Influence on Early Childhood Education."
     A.   Jean Piaget
     B.   Maria Montessori
     C.   Jean-Jacques Rousseau
     D.   John Dewey

5.   The development of the psychosocial theory is attributed to which of the following theorists?
     Hint: See "Historical Figures and Their Influence on Early Childhood Education."
     A.   Abraham Maslow
     B.   Erik Erikson
     C.   Jean Piaget
     D.   Jean-Jacques Rousseau

6.   Friedrich Froebel's contributions to contemporary early childhood education do <u>not</u> include which of the following?
     Hint: See "Historical Figures and Their Influence on Early Childhood Education."
     A.   Established the first teacher's college for early childhood educators
     B.   The importance of learning through play
     C.   Gifts and occupations
     D.   The important role of the teacher in planning the learning environment

7.   Maria Montessori was a _____ who worked primarily with children who were
     _____.
     Hint: See "Historical Figures and Their Influence on Early Childhood Education."
     A.   Mathematician, gifted.
     B.   Physician, medically fragile.
     C.   Mathematician, developmentally delayed.
     D.   Physician, mentally retarded.

8.   Vygotsky believed learning is supported and enhanced by others through social interaction. Which of the following is <u>not</u> an important concept in Vygotsky's theory?
     Hint: See "Historical Figures and Their Influence on Early Childhood Education."
     A.   The zone of proximal development
     B.   Interpersonal interactions
     C.   Scaffolding
     D.   Schemes

9. Howard Gardner has played an important role in helping educators rethink the concept of intelligence. Which of the following theories is attributed to Gardner?
   Hint: **See "Historical Figures and Their Influence on Early Childhood Education."**
   A. Theory of multiple intelligences
   B. Theory of psychosocial development
   C. Theory of cognitive development
   D. Theory of cultural literacy

10. In Piaget's theory of cognitive development the stages are_____.
    Hint: **See "Historical Figures and Their Influence on Early Childhood Education."**
    A. The same for all children.
    B. Different for atypical children.
    C. Fixed by age—the age a child goes through a stage does not vary.
    D. Varied by the sequence—each child will go through a different sequence of stages.

11. Which of the following statements is <u>not</u> a belief based on the children as persons with rights view?
    Hint: **See "Views of Children Through the Ages."**
    A. Children's rights need to be defined, promoted, and defended.
    B. Children are miniature adults with similar rights.
    C. Health and economic well-being are essential to political freedoms and rights.
    D. Fetal rights are protected at the state and federal level.

12. Which of the following best defines child-centered education?
    Hint: **See "Child-Centered Education"**
    A. Children can learn all that they need to know if they are left to their own devices in a nurturing environment.
    B. Children are passive participants in their education and development.
    C. All children are unique and are active participants in their education and development.
    D. All children are unique and learn best if they are left to their own devices in a nurturing environment.

Discussion Questions

1. Discuss the reasons why it is important to know about the great educators who have influenced the field of early childhood education.

2. Identify five great educators from the past and explain their contributions to current practice in early childhood education.

3. Discuss child-centered education. How will the guidelines for child-centered education influence your classroom practice?

CHAPTER 5

THEORIES APPLIED TO TEACHING AND LEARNING: FOUNDATIONS FOR PRACTICE

I. <u>Chapter Objectives</u>

<u>Learner outcomes</u>

The learner will
- Explain the importance of Piaget's theory of cognitive development
- Identify the cognitive processes Piaget considered important for intellectual development
- Identify and explain the sociocultural theory of Vygotsky
- Explain the self-actualization theory of Maslow
- Explain the key ideas of Erickson, Gardner, and Bronfenbrenner

II. <u>Chapter Overview</u>

What are theories of behavior and learning, and why are they important?

What are the major features of the theories of Piaget, Vygotsky, Maslow, Bronfenbrenner, Erickson, and Gardner?

How can you use theories of learning in your professional practice?

III.   **Chapter 5 Study Guide**

Directions: As you read the chapter, answer the following questions. Use the guide to study the chapter information.

Theories of Learning and Development

1.   Define *learning*_____

_____

_____

       Define *theory*_____

_____

_____

2.   Learning theories are important for several reasons. Identify the four reasons listed in your book:

       a. _____

       _____

       b. _____

       _____

       c. _____

       _____

       d. _____

       _____

Piaget's Theory of Learning

3.   Describe how Piaget viewed intelligence. See text page 113.

       _____

       _____

       _____

       _____

4.   Define *constructivism.*

_____

_____

_____

What are the basic concepts of constructivism?

a.
b.
c.
d.
e.

What are the characteristics of a constructivist classroom?

a.	b.
c.	d.
e.	f.
g.	h.
i.	j.

5.   Describe active learning.

_____

_____

_____

6.   According to Piaget, learning is a form of adaptation. The following terms are important in understanding the adaptive process. Define each term and give appropriate examples of each.

Adaptation: _____

_____

_____

_____

_____

Assimilation: _____

_____

_____

_____

_____

Accommodation: _____

_____

_____

_____

_____

Equilibrium: _____

_____

_____

_____

_____

Schemes: _____

_____

_____

_____

_____

7.   Use the box to identify the key elements of Piaget's stages of intellectual development.

Piaget's Stages of Intellectual Development

Stage	Characteristics
Sensorimotor (birth to two years)	
Preoperational (two to seven years)	
Concrete Operations (seven to twelve years)	

Lev Vygotsky and Sociocultural Theory

8.   What is the zone of proximal development?

_____

_____

_____

What is intersubjectivity?

_____

_____

_____

_____

_____

What is scaffolding?

_____

_____

_____

_____

Abraham Maslow and Self-Actualization Theory

9.   What is self-actualization?

_____

_____

_____

_____

10.   List and describe the six basic needs identified in Maslow's Hierarchy of Needs:

a. _____

_____

b. _____

_____

c. _____

_____

d. _____

_____

e. _____

_____

f. _____

_____

Erik Erikson

11.   Use the box to describe Erikson's stages of psychosocial development in early childhood.

Erikson's Stages of Psychosocial Development

Stage	Characteristics
Basic Trust versus Mistrust (birth to eighteen months)	
Autonomy versus Shame and Doubt (eighteen months to three years)	
Initiative versus Guilt (three to five years)	
Industry versus Inferiority (five to eight years)	

Howard Gardner

12.   Review Howard Gardner's theory of multiple intelligences. Identify the eight
       intelligences and provide an example of each.

Gardner's Theory of Multiple Intelligences

Intelligence	Example
1.	
2.	
3.	
4.	
5.	
6.	
7.	
8.	

Urie Bronfenbrenner and Ecological Theory

13.   What is the ecological theory?

_____

_____

_____

_____

_____

14. Identify and explain the five interrelating environmental systems of the ecological theory.

Microsystem: _____

_____

_____

_____

_____

Mesosystem: _____

_____

_____

_____

_____

Exosystem: _____

_____

_____

_____

_____

Macrosystem: _____

_____

_____

_____

_____

Chronosystem: _____

_____

_____

_____

_____

Theories Reconsidered

15. What are the advantages and disadvantages regarding Piaget's theory of cognitive development?

Advantages	Disadvantages
a.	a.
b.	b.
c.	c.
d.	d.

16. Explain the importance of the work of Vygotsky, Erickson, and Bronfenbrenner.

_____

_____

_____

_____

_____

_____

17. Identify and explain the two new discoveries that may modify how we think about cognitive development.

_____

_____

_____

_____

_____

IV.   Making Connections

Locate the articles below on the Internet. Read both articles. Write a reflection detailing how you can use the ideas in your own classroom. Be prepared to share the reflection with your class.

Is It Constructivism?
http://www.sedl.org/pubs/sedletter/v09n03/construct.html

The Practice Implications of Constructivism
http://www.sedl.org/pubs/sedletter/v09n03/practice.html

V.   Chapter 5 Self-Check

Multiple Choice Questions Select the best answer.

1.   The ability to reverse operations and to conserve usually indicates that the child is functioning at which of the following stages of development?
     Hint: **See "Piaget's Theory of Learning."**
     A.   Sensorimotor stage
     B.   Preoperational stage
     C.   Concrete operations stage
     D.   Formal operations stage

2.   In Piaget's theory of cognitive development the stages are:
     Hint: **See "Piaget's Theory of Learning."**
     A.   The same for all children.
     B.   Different for atypical children.
     C.   Fixed by age— the age a child goes through a stage does not vary.
     D.   Varied by the sequence— each child will go through a different sequence of stages.

3. Which of the following is not a characteristic of the sensorimotor period of development?
   Hint: **See "Piaget's Theory of Learning."**
   A. Dependency on innate reflexive actions
   B. Initial development of object permanence
   C. Egocentricity where the child is the center of the world and believes events are caused by them
   D. Representational thinking

4. In the concrete operations stage of cognitive development, the early childhood professional should do all of the following <u>except</u>:
   Hint: **See "Piaget's Theory of Learning."**
   A. Remember that telling is not teaching.
   B. Structure learning so children have experiences at their level with real objects, things and people.
   C. Provide many abstract activities that require the child to think.
   D. Remember that children need mental and physical activity for cognitive development.

5. Learning theories are important for all the following reasons <u>except</u>:
   Hint: **See "Theories of Learning and Development."**
   A. They provide guidance in developing programs for children that support their learning.
   B. They provide the exact ages that a child needs to learn specific information.
   C. They enable early childhood professionals to explain to parents how learning occurs.
   D. They provide a basis for evaluating children's learning.

6. According to Piaget, intelligence means:
   Hint: **See "Piaget's Theory of Learning."**
   A. The IQ measured on an intelligence test
   B. The mental abilities of the child
   C. The cognitive or mental process by which a child acquires knowledge
   D. The mental capacity of the child for learning

7. According to Vygotsky, learning is supported and enhanced by others through social interaction. Which of the following is <u>not</u> an important concept in Vygotsky's theory?
   Hint: **See "Lev Vygotsky and Sociocultural Theory."**
   A. The zone of proximal development
   B. Interpersonal interactions
   C. Scaffolding
   D. Schemes

8. The theory of psychosocial development is attributed to which of the following?
   Hint: **See "Erik Erikson."**
   A. Abraham Maslow
   B. Erik Erikson
   C. Jean Piaget
   D. Howard Gardner

9. Abraham Maslow's theory of self-actualization is based on the satisfaction of human needs. Maslow identified self-actualization as the highest human need. Which of the following is the most accurate description of the basic needs that must be satisfied for a person to reach self-actualization?
   Hint: **See "Abraham Maslow and Self-Actualization Theory."**
   A. Food, safety, security
   B. Life essentials, safety and security, belongingness and love, achievement and prestige, aesthetic needs
   C. Food, safety and love, achievement and prestige
   D. Life essentials, belongingness, and achievement

10. Howard Gardner has played an important role in helping educators rethink the concept of intelligence. Which of the following theories is attributed to Gardner?
    Hint: **See "Howard Gardner."**
    A. Theory of multiple intelligences
    B. Theory of psychosocial development
    C. Theory of cognitive development
    D. Theory of cultural literacy

11. Which of the following are included in Bronfenbrenner's ecological theory?
    Hint: **See "Urie Bronfenbrenner and Ecological Theory."**
    A. Microsystem, ecosystem, and exosystem
    B. Mesosystem, exosystem, and chronosystem
    C. Exosystem, ecosystem, and chronosystem
    D. None of the above

12. According to _____, children's personalities and social skills grow and develop within the context of society and in response to society's demands, expectations, values, and social institutions such as families, schools, and child care programs.
    Hint: **See "Urie Bronfenbrenner and Ecological Theory."**
    A. Jean Piaget
    B. Urie Bronfenbrenner
    C. Howard Gardner
    D. Erik Erikson

Discussion Questions

1. Explain the term *equilibrium*. Children will reject new information if the new ideas are radically different from past experiences. Describe a situation where the child rejects new information and tell how this relates to the idea of equilibrium.

2. Define and explain the influence of the ecological theory on child development.

3. Discuss the advantages and criticisms of Piaget's theory of cognitive development.

CHAPTER 6

EARLY CHILDHOOD PROGRAMS: APPLYING THEORIES TO PRACTICE

I. <u>**Chapter Objectives**</u>

<u>**Learner outcomes**</u>

The learner will
- Explain the need for high-quality early childhood education programs
- Identify the features of high-quality early childhood education programs
- Identify and explain the characteristics of the Montessori, High/Scope, and Reggio Emilia programs
- Determine the implications early childhood programs have for your practice as an early childhood professional

II. <u>**Chapter Overview**</u>

Why is there a need for high-quality early childhood education programs?

What are the basic features of high-quality early childhood education programs?

What are the unique characteristics and strengths of early childhood education programs?

How can you apply features of early childhood programs to your professional practice?

III. **Chapter 6 Study Guide**

Directions: As you read the chapter, answer the following questions. Use the guide to study the chapter information.

The Growing Demand for Quality Early Childhood Programs

1. What is the National Association for the Education of Young Children (NAEYC)? What is the role of NAEYC in early childhood programs?

_____

_____

_____

_____

_____

_____

_____

2. Identify three public demands of early childhood professionals:

    a. _____

    _____

    _____

    b. _____

    _____

    _____

    c. _____

    _____

    _____

3.   Compare the main features of the four programs discussed in Chapter 6.

High/Scope	Reggio Emilia	Montessori	Waldorf

Principles of the Montessori Method

4.   Describe the teacher's role in the Montessori classroom.

_____

_____

_____

_____

_____

_____

_____

_____

_____

_____

5.   Identify the basic principles of the Montessori approach. Use the chart to record the key elements of the Montessori approach.

Principles of the Montessori Approach

Respect for the child
The absorbent mind
Sensitive periods
Prepared environment
Autoeducation

How Does the Montessori Method Work?

6.   What are the three basic areas of child involvement in Montessori's prepared environment?

_____

_____

_____

7.   What are practical life activities and what is the purpose of those activities?

_____

_____

_____

_____

_____

_____

8.   List at least six sensory materials found in typical Montessori classrooms:

a.	b.
c.	d.
e.	f.

9.   Explain the basic purposes of sensory materials.

_____

_____

_____

_____

_____

_____

_____

_____

_____

_____

10. Identify the Montessori approach to writing, reading, and mathematics and examples of materials used for each content area. Use the box below to record this information.

Approach	Materials
Writing:	
Reading:	
Mathematics:	

Montessori and Contemporary Practices

11. The Montessori approach supports many methods used in contemporary early childhood programs. List and define the six methods identified in the text:

a. _____

_____

_____

b. _____

_____

_____

c. _____

_____

_____

d. _____

_____

_____

e. _____

_____

_____

f. _____

_____

_____

High/Scope: A Constructivist Approach

12. What are the three fundamental principles of the High/Scope model?

_____

_____

_____

_____

_____

13. Identify the goals of the High/Scope approach.

_____

_____

_____

_____

_____

14. What are the key elements of the High/Scope approach?

Key Elements of the High/Scope Program

a.
b.
c.
d.
e.

15. What is the High/Scope daily routine?

Planning Time: _____

_____

_____

_____

Key Experiences: _____

_____

_____

Work Time: _____

_____

_____

_____

Cleanup Time: _____

_____

_____

_____

Recall Time: _____

_____

_____

_____

16. Identify three advantages to implementing the High/Scope approach.

_____

_____

_____

_____

_____

_____

_____

Reggio Emilia

17.   What is Reggio Emilia?

_____

_____

_____

18.   What considerations must early childhood professionals make when considering the Reggio Emilia approach?

_____

_____

_____

19.   What should early childhood professionals keep in mind when considering the Reggio Emilia approach?

_____

_____

_____

_____

_____

_____

20.   Using the chart below, identify the basic principles of Reggio Emilia approach.

Basic Principles of Reggio Emilia

Beliefs About Children and How They Learn
a. Relationships

b. Time

Adult's Role
a. The teacher

b. The atelierista

c. Parents

The Environment
a. The physical space

b. The atelier

Program Practices
a. Documentation

b. Curriculum and practices

21. All of the programs described in the text have unique features but they all have the common goal of a good quality education for young children. Use the following chart to list the unique features of each of the programs discussed.

Early Childhood Program Analysis

Program	Theory	Classroom Activity	What I Like About the Program
High/Scope			
Reggio Emilia			
Montessori			
Waldorf			

IV. Making Connections

The High/Scope Perry Preschool Study is the most comprehensive study of early intervention programs on record to date. Go to the web site and read the results of the study.

Summary of Significant Benefits
http://www.highscope.org/Research/PerryProject/perrymain.htm

What do you think about the results? Were there any surprising findings? What implications do the results suggest for early childhood professionals?

Be prepared to discuss your findings in class.

V.   **Chapter 6 Self-Check**

Multiple Choice Questions Select the best answer.

1.   The United States is once again discovering the importance of the early years. Which of the following is <u>not</u> one of the demands of the public for quality early childhood programs?
       Hint: See **"The Growing Demand for Quality Early Childhood Programs."**
       A.   Programs that will help ensure children's early academic and school success
       B.   The inclusion of early literacy and reading readiness activities that will enable children to read on grade level in grades 1, 2, and 3
       C.   Programs that exclude parents from the decision-making process in education
       D.   Environments that will help children develop the social and behavioral skills necessary to help them lead nonviolent lives

2.   The Montessori approach is based on which of the following principles?
       Hint: See **"Principles of the Montessori Method."**
       A.   Respect for the child
       B.   The absorbent mind
       C.   Sensitive periods
       D.   All of the above

3.   According to Montessori, there are conscious and unconscious stages in the development of the absorbent mind. During which of the following stages does the unconscious absorbent mind develop the senses?
       Hint: See **"Principles of the Montessori Method."**
       A.   From birth to three years
       B.   From three to six years
       C.   From birth to eight years
       D.   From six to eight years

4.   Montessori programs are popular with parents. Which of the following is <u>not</u> a reason for the popularity of the Montessori approach?
       Hint: See **"Principles of the Montessori Method."**
       A.   Montessori education has always been identified as quality education for young children.
       B.   Montessori programs are not available in public schools.
       C.   Parents who observe a good Montessori program like the orderliness and calm environment of the program.
       D.   In Montessori programs the child is at the center of the learning process.

5.   The prepared environment emphasizes practical activities such as carrying trays and chairs, greeting a visitor, and learning self-care skills. These activities include polishing mirrors, sweeping floors, and dusting furniture. Montessori believed that _____.
      Hint: **See "The Prepared Environment."**
      A.   Children need to know how to clean up the classroom.
      B.   Teachers should tell children exactly how to do the sweeping and dusting so they will know how to complete the task successfully.
      C.   Involvement and concentration in motor activities help make the child independent of the adult and develop concentration.
      D.   Children should be made to polish shoes or scrub tables for at least twenty minutes in order to clean them properly.

6.   Sensory materials are an important part of a Montessori classroom. Sensory materials include smelling jars, color tablets, sound boxes, and cloth swatches, to name a few. Which of the following is not one of the characteristics of materials for training and developing the senses?
      Hint: **See "Sensory Materials."**
      A.   Materials are designed so that children can see if they make a mistake.
      B.   Materials encourage active involvement rather than the more passive process of looking.
      C.   Materials are designed so that the child may explore many qualities at one time.
      D.   Materials are attractive, with colors and proportions that appeal to children.

7.   The High/Scope educational approach is based on Piaget's cognitive developmental theory. Which of the following is not one of the three fundamental principles of High/Scope?
      Hint: **See "High/Scope: A Constructivist Approach."**
      A.   Active participation of children in choosing and evaluating learning activities
      B.   Regular daily planning
      C.   Regular daily testing to assess progress toward program goals
      D.   Developmentally sequenced goals and materials for children based on "key experiences"

8.   Professionals who use the High/Scope curriculum must create a context for learning by implementing and supporting five essential elements. Which of the following is not one of the five essential elements of the High/Scope approach?
      Hint: **See "The Five Elements of the High/Scope Approach."**
      A.   Classroom arrangement
      B.   Passive learning
      C.   The daily schedule
      D.   Assessment

9.   Reggio Emelia, a city in northern Italy, is widely known for its approach to educating young children. All of the following are beliefs of the Reggio schools about children and how they learn except _____.
        Hint: See **"Beliefs About Children and How They Learn."**
        A.   Just as Vygotsky believed, individualism is valued over relationships.
        B.   Time is not set by the clock or a calendar but by the children's own sense of time and their personal rhythm.
        C.   Parents have the right to be involved in the life of the school, and teachers have the right to grow professionally.
        D.   Teachers must observe and listen closely to children to know how to plan or proceed with their work.

10.   The theoretical base of the Reggio Emilia approach includes:
        Hint: See **"Reggio Emilia."**
        A.   Piaget, Froebel, Hirsch, and Montessori
        B.   Piaget, Montessori, and Gardner
        C.   Piaget, Vygotsky, Dewey, and Montessori
        D.   Piaget, Vygotsky, Dewey, and Gardner

11.   Waldorf education can be described using which of the following three words?
        Hint: See **"Waldorf Education: Head, Hands, and Heart."**
        A.   Mind, music, movement
        B.   Cognition, creativity, competition
        C.   Intelligence, imagination, independence
        D.   Head, Hands, Heart

12.   According to Steiner and the Waldorf education movement, anthroposophy is defined as _____.
        Hint: See **"Waldorf Education: Head, Hands, and Heart."**
        A.   The art of movement.
        B.   The study of folk and fairy tales, fables, and legends.
        C.   The science of the spirit.
        D.   Respect for the child's processes of development and their developmental stages.

Discussion Questions

1.   Discuss the academic component of Montessori's approach to learning, including reading, writing, and mathematics.

2.   Describe the High/Scope approach to early childhood education.

3.   Discuss the Reggio Emilia approach to early education and the considerations for implementing the approach in an American setting.

CHAPTER 7

CHILD CARE: MEETING THE NEEDS OF CHILDREN, PARENTS, AND FAMILIES

I.   **Chapter Objectives**

Learner outcomes

The learner will
- Explain why early childhood education models are needed
- Identify the basic features of early childhood education models
- Compare and contrast the similarities, differences, and strengths of early childhood education models
- Determine the implications the program models have for your practice as an early childhood professional

II.   **Chapter Overview**

Why is there a need for child care services?

What are the types of child care offered today?

What constitutes quality in child care programs?

How effective is child care in meeting the needs of children and families?

What are significant issues surrounding child care and its use?

III. **Chapter 7 Study Guide**

Directions: As you read the chapter, answer the following questions. Use the guide to study the chapter information.

What Is Child Care?

1. Child care is a comprehensive service to children and families that supplements the care and education that children receive from their families. Child care programs do the following:

    a. _____

    _____

    b. _____

    _____

    c. _____

    _____

    d. _____

    _____

    e. _____

    _____

2. List a few of the reasons for the popularity of child care.

    _____

    _____

    _____

    _____

    _____

    _____

    _____

3.   Review the facts about child care on text page 179. Identify the three facts that you find most surprising or interesting.

_____

_____

_____

_____

Types of Child Care Programs

4.   Briefly describe each type of child care program listed in the boxes below.

Child Care Programs

Child Care by Relatives and Friends	Family Child Care
Intergenerational Child Care	Center-Based Child Care
Employer-Sponsored Child Care	Proprietary Child Care
Backup Child Care	Military Child Care
Before-School and After-School Care	

What Constitutes Quality Education and Care?

5.   Explain each of the following main characteristics of quality child care programs.

Appropriate and safe environments
Caregiver-child ratio
Developmentally appropriate programs
Individual needs
Culturally appropriate practice
Family education and support
Staff training and development
Program accreditation

The Effects of Care and Education on Children

6. Summarize the longitudinal study of the National Institute of Child Health and Human Development (NICHD).

_____

_____

_____

_____

_____

_____

_____

7. According to the results of the NICHD study, what are some of the lasting benefits of high-quality child care?

a. _____

_____

b. _____

_____

c. _____

_____

d. _____

_____

e. _____

_____

f. _____

_____

IV.   **Making Connections**

The National Child Care Information Center provides information and articles on child care. Go to the web site and view the PowerPoint about quality care and licensing trends.

A Foundation for Quality Care: A Look at Child Care Licensing Regulations, Trends and Current Issues
http://www.naccrra.org/docs/symp2004/media/7.ppt#11

Identify three statistics that you find surprising. Be prepared to discuss your concerns in class.

V.   **Chapter 7 Self-Check**

Multiple Choice Questions Select the best answer.

1.   Child care is the focus of public attention for which of the following reasons?
        Hint: See "What Is Child Care?"
        A.   Demographic changes have created a high demand for child care.
        B.   There are more dual-income families.
        C.   Child care is viewed by many politicians as a solution to the nation's economic and social problems.
        D.   All of the above.

2.   When child care is provided in a family-like setting it is known as _____.
        Hint: See "Types of Child Care Programs."
        A.   Family child care.
        B.   Intergenerational child care.
        C.   Proprietary child care.
        D.   Not for profit child care.

3.   The Children's Defense Fund (CDF) focuses primarily on which series of issues?
        Hint: See "Children's Defense Fund: Advocating for Children at the National Level."
        A.   Licensing, abuse and neglect, and child poverty.
        B.   Child care, preschool, and after-school activities.
        C.   Child care, after-school activities, and child poverty.
        D.   Licensing, preschool, and child care.

4.   Which of the following is not a component of quality child care?
        Hint: See "What Constitutes Quality Care and Education?"
        A.   Incorporates practices reflecting the values and beliefs of families and cultures of the community.
        B.   Licensing ensures that a child care setting meets basic health and safety requirements.
        C.   All child care providers have the minimum of an associate's degree.
        D.   Learning is an interactive process that involves opportunities for exploration and interactions.

5. Research has shown that when child care programs meet the recommended child-staff ratios and levels of caregiver education, children have better outcomes. What is the NAEYC recommended ratio of caregivers to children in a program for infants?
    Hint: **See "Caregiver-Child Ratio."**
    A. 1:3 or 1:4
    B. 1:4 or 1:5
    C. 1:5 or 1:6
    D. 1:6 or 1:7

6. There are many options for child care. What three issues are always a part of the child care landscape?
    Hint: **See "Types of Child Care Programs."**
    A. Education, affordability, and accessibility
    B. Quality, affordability, and accessibility
    C. Quality, education, and affordability
    D. Affordability, accessibility, and services

7. Quality programs use developmentally appropriate practices to implement the curriculum and achieve their program goals. Developmentally appropriate programs include education to meet the _____.
    Hint: **See "Developmentally Appropriate Programs."**
    A. Physical and cognitive needs of all children.
    B. Social, emotional, and cognitive needs of all children.
    C. Social and emotional needs of all children.
    D. Physical and social needs of all children.

8. Child care that is conducted in specially renovated, constructed areas in churches, YMCAs, and other such facilities is _____.
    Hint: **See "Types of Child Care Programs."**
    A. Intergenerational child care.
    B. Center-based child care.
    C. Employer-sponsored child care.
    D. Proprietary child care.

9. The NICHD Study of Early Child Care (SECC) found that high-quality early care and education have influences that last over a lifetime. Children who attend high-quality programs experience all of the following <u>except</u> _____.
    Hint: **See "The Effects of Care and Education on Children."**
    I.   Higher cognitive performance of children in child care.
    II.   Higher academic achievement in both reading and math.
    III. Better scores in math ability than children in low-quality care.
    IV.   More years of education completed and a greater likelihood to attend a four-year college.
    A. I, II, and IV
    B. I, III, and IV
    C. I, II, III, and IV
    D. I and IV only

10. Child care is a billion dollar industry, and for-profit child care organizations are growing in number and size. Which of the following child care management organizations have the largest number of contracted centers in the United States?
    Hint: **See "Largest Child Care Management Organizations in the United States."**
    A.   La Petite Academy
    B.   Bright Horizons Family Solutions
    C.   KinderCare Learning Centers
    D.   Knowledge Learning Corporation

11. According to the National Study of Before and After School Programs, about 1.7 million and children in kindergarten through grade eight and are enrolled in 49,500 programs. The most common sponsors of before- and after-school child care are _____.
    Hint: **See "Before-and After-School Care."**
    A.   Public schools, for-profit corporations, and nonprofit organizations.
    B.   Public schools, for-profit corporations, and church groups.
    C.   For-profit corporations, federal grants, and church groups.
    D.   Public schools, church groups, local agencies.

12. What percent of mothers with children under three are employed?
    Hint: **See "The Popularity of Child Care"**
    A.   62.3%
    B.   54.1%
    C.   53.9%
    D.   62.1%

Discussion Questions

1. Discuss the benefits of high-quality child care and education of young children.

2. Describe the types of child care and consider the families that seek each type of care.

3. Quality programs use developmentally appropriate practices to implement the curriculum. Describe some of the methods these quality programs use to meet the social, emotional, and cognitive needs of all children.

CHAPTER 8

THE FEDERAL GOVERNMENT: SUPPORTING CHILDREN'S SUCCESS

I. **Chapter Objectives**

Learner outcomes

The learner will
- Explain the involvement of federal agencies in early childhood programs
- Describe the role of federal agencies in transforming early childhood education
- Describe the purpose of federal programs that serve young children and their families
- Explain the funding issues involved in early childhood programs

II. **Chapter Overview**

Why are federal agencies so involved in programs that support and educate children and families?

How are federal agencies transforming early childhood education?

What are the essential purposes of federal programs that serve young children and their families?

What are basic issues involved in the federal funding and control of early childhood programs?

III. Chapter 8 Study Guide

Directions: As you read the chapter, answer the following questions. Use the guide to study the chapter information.

Federal Legislation and Early Childhood

1.   What is the No Child Left Behind Act of 2001 (NCLB Act)?

_____

_____

_____

_____

_____

2.   What has been put in place to ensure that every child can read on grade level by the end of third grade?

_____

_____

_____

_____

3.   Identify some of the federal programs that support early care and education for children and families. See Figure 8.1 in your text.

_____

_____

_____

_____

Head Start and Early Head Start

4.   What is the history and purpose of Head Start?

_____

_____

_____

_____

_____

_____

5.   What are the five objectives for Head Start?

_____

_____

_____

_____

_____

6.   Head Start and Early Head Start are required to comply with federal performance standards. List the ten of the performance standards:

a.	b.
c.	d.
e.	f.
g.	h.
i.	j.

7. The implementation of the standards of learning or indicators support local Head Start efforts in their compliance of the federal performance standards. List the nine standards of learning or indicators:

a. _____

b. _____

c. _____

d. _____

e. _____

f. _____

g. _____

h. _____

i. _____

8. Good Start, Grow Smart helps state and local communities strengthen early learning for young children. The Good Start, Grow Smart initiative addresses three major areas. Describe each of the three areas in the boxes provided.

Strengthening Head Start	Partnering with States	Providing Information

9. What is the history and purpose of Early Head Start?

_____

_____

_____

10. What are the three objectives for Early Head Start?

_____

_____

_____

11. Head Start and Early Head Start have the flexibility to structure their programs to meet the needs of the children, families, and communities they serve. Briefly describe each of the four options in the boxes provided.

Center-based option
Home-based option
Combination option
Local option

12.a. What criteria must be met for a child to be eligible for Head Start?

_____

_____

_____

_____

b. What criteria must be met for families to be eligible for Early Head Start?

_____

_____

_____

Other Programs

13.   There are other programs that operate with a mission similar to Head Start and Early Head Start. Using the chart below, define the program, describe the unique characteristics of the program, and give examples of the program.

Program	Definition	Characteristics	Examples
Migrant Head Start			
American Indian–Alaska Native Head Start Programs			
Even Start Family Literacy Program			
Title I Programs			

Fatherhood Initiatives

14.   Identify the principles that guide the Department of Health and Human Services' special fatherhood initiatives:

a. _____

_____

b. _____

_____

c. _____

_____

d. _____

_____

e. _____

_____

Partnerships and Collaboration

15.   Head Start Programs endeavor to develop and build collaborative relationships with local agencies and programs. Describe a collaborative program and explain its purpose as detailed in your text.

_____

_____

_____

_____

_____

_____

Head Start Research

16.   According to the body of research, do Head Start, Early Head Start, and Even Start programs deliver the services they were authorized and funded to deliver, and do these services make a difference in the lives of children and families? Explain and give examples.

_____

_____

_____

_____

17.	As with all programs, Head Start has associated issues of concern. Some of these concerns are making Head Start a center for national attention. Describe these concerns in the boxes provided.

Accountability
Testing Head Start Children
Federal Control and Influence
National Curriculum
Improving Teacher Quality

## IV.	__Making Connections__

Go to the following web site to learn more about the No Child Left Behind Act of 2001. How do you think the No Child Left Behind Act will affect your early childhood career? Identify at least three ways you believe this will affect your classroom and explain why. Be prepared to share your ideas in class.

Introduction and Overview: No Child Left Behind
http://www.nclb.gov/next/overview/index.html

V. **Chapter 8 Self-Check**

Multiple Choice Questions: Select the best answer.

1. Federal legislation has had an influence on the educational process at all levels. For early childhood education, the passage of the _____ marks the beginning of contemporary federal political and financial support.
   Hint: **See "Federal Legislation and Early Childhood."**
   A. No Child Left Behind Act of 2001
   B. Reading First Act of 1999
   C. Goals 2000, Educate America Act of 1994
   D. Economic Opportunity Act of 1964

2. _____ programs are programs and services children and families are entitled to because they meet the eligibility criteria for the services. Head Start and Early Head Start are examples of this type of program.
   Hint: **See "Federal Programs and Early Education."**
   A. Mandated
   B. Entitlement
   C. Early Childhood
   D. Public

3. Head Start was implemented in 1965. The first programs were designed for which of the following reasons?
   Hint: **See "Head Start."**
   A. To give children who did not attend kindergarten a "head start" on their first-grade experience
   B. To give all children who spoke English as a second language a "head start" on their public school experience
   C. To give children from low-income families who did not attend kindergarten a "head start" on their first-grade experience
   D. To give children who did not do well in kindergarten a "head start" on their first-grade experience

4. Head Start is based on the premise that all children share certain needs and that children of low-income families in particular can benefit from a comprehensive developmental program to meet those needs. Which of the following is an objective of Head Start?
   Hint: **See "Head Start."**
   A. Enhance children's growth and development
   B. Strengthen families as the primary nurturers of their children
   C. Provide children with educational, health, and nutritional services
   D. All of the above are objectives of Head Start

5. Which of the following is <u>not</u> an outcome identified in the Head Start Child Outcomes Framework?

    Hint: **See "Figure 8.3, Head Start Child Outcomes Framework."**

    A. Develops increasing ability to count to ten and beyond.
    B. Shows increasing awareness of print in the classroom, home, and community settings.
    C. Identifies twenty-six uppercase letters.
    D. Develops understanding that writing is a way of communicating for a variety of purposes.

6. Good Start, Grow Smart helps state and local communities strengthen early learning for young children. Which of the following are the three major initiatives of Good Start, Grow Smart?

    Hint: **See "Good Start, Grow Smart."**

    A. Strengthen Head Start, partner with states to improve early childhood education, and promote family literacy
    B. Strengthen Head Start, promote family literacy, and provide information to teachers, caregivers, and parents
    C. Coordinate family services, strengthen Head Start, and provide information to teachers, caregivers, and parents
    D. Strengthen Head Start, partner with states to improve early childhood education, and provide information to teachers, caregivers, and parents

7. Which of the following is <u>not</u> a program service offered by Early Head Start?

    Hint: **See "Early Head Start."**

    A. Parenting education
    B. Career counseling
    C. Nutrition education
    D. Family support services

8. All of the following are Head Start programs that serve special populations <u>except</u>:

    Hint: **See "Other Head Start Programs."**

    A. Migrant Head Start
    B. Even Start Family Literacy Program
    C. High/Scope programs
    D. American Indian–Alaska Native Head Start Programs

9. The No Child Left Behind Act of 2001 reauthorized the Elementary and Secondary Education Act (ESEA) of 1965. Under this reauthorization, Title I provides what type of assistance to state educational agencies, local educational agencies, and schools with high numbers or percentages of poor children?

    Hint: **See "Title I Programs."**

    A. Financial
    B. Standards of quality for early elementary programs
    C. Staff development and training
    D. None of the above

10. A Parent Advisory Committee is an important part of Title I schools. The committee meets three times a year to review which of the following?
    Hint: **See "Title I – Helping Children Become Lifelong Learners."**
    A.   Schoolwide plan, the budget, and the discipline plan
    B.   The discipline plan, the after-school program, and the budget
    C.   Schoolwide plan, staff development plan, and the safety plan
    D.   Schoolwide plan, the budget, and parent-school compacts

11. Under the provisions of Good Start, Grow Smart, the preschool initiative of NCLB every _____ in Head Start is now tested with the Head Start National Reporting System.
    Hint: **See "Testing Head Start Children."**
    A.   Three-year-old
    B.   Four-year-old
    C.   Non-native speaker of English
    D.   Native speaker of English

12. As with all programs, Head Start has associated issues of concern. Which of the following is not an issue of concern?
    Hint: **See "Head Start Research."**
    A.   Accountability
    B.   Testing of children
    C.   Declining enrollment
    D.   Improving teacher quality

Discussion Questions

1. What is Head Start and what is the significance of the Head Start programs?

2. Identify and explain the Early Head Start program. What is the difference between Head Start and Early Head Start?

3. What is the fatherhood initiative? Explain the purpose of the fatherhood initiative.

CHAPTER 9

INFANTS AND TODDLERS: FOUNDATION YEARS FOR LEARNING

I. **Chapter Objectives**

Learner outcomes

The learner will
- Explain how research is influencing the care and education of infants and toddlers
- Identify milestones in infant and toddler development
- Apply Piaget's cognitive theory to infant and toddler development
- Identify the theories that explain infant and toddler language and development
- Apply Erickson's theory of psychosocial development to infant and toddler development
- Analyze the components of quality programs for infants and toddlers

II. **Chapter Overview**

How is research influencing the care and education of infants and toddlers?

What are the key milestones in infant and toddler development?

How do theories of development explain infant and toddler cognitive, language, and psychosocial development?

How can you and other professionals provide quality programs for infants and toddlers?

III.   Chapter 9 Study Guide

Directions: As you read the chapter, answer the following questions. Use the guide to study to study the chapter information.

Culture and Child Development

1.   Define *culture*.

    _____

    _____

    _____

2.   Child rearing practices are influenced by culture. Think for a moment how culture can influence parental and caregiver practices in the following routines that affect children's developmental outcomes, and describe the influences in the boxes provided.

Practice	Influences
Bottle or Breast Feeding	
Feeding Solid Foods	
Toileting	
Napping	
Use of Comfort Items	

What Are Infants and Toddlers Like?

3.   Infancy is the period of growth and development covering children ages _____ to _____. Toddlerhood is the period of growth and development covering children ages _____ to _____.

4.   Understanding the major developmental processes that characterize the early years will help early childhood professionals provide quality care and education for infants and toddlers. Answer the following questions identified in your text using the Portraits of Infants and Toddlers.

Review Oliver's and Conner's portraits. What is a common theme in their cognitive development?

_____

_____

_____

Review Marisa's and Hyato's portraits. How might classrooms need to be adjusted for the Hispanic and Laotian cultures?

_____

_____

_____

_____

Review Joseph's and Mariafe's portraits. How can you accommodate the different adaptive needs of toddlers in the classroom?

_____

_____

_____

_____

Review Christy's and Daniel's portraits. Do all two-year-olds need the same level of supervision? What kinds of unique supervision might Christy and Daniel need?

_____

_____

_____

Young Brains: A Primer

5.   Brain research has created a great deal of interest in the first three years of life. Complete the following table to identify facts and definitions about the young brain.

Brain Facts and Definitions

Brain Weight Birth: Six months: Two years: Adult:	
Amount of neurons at birth:	
Shearing or Pruning:	
Synapses are:	
Synaptogenesis is:	
Sensitive periods are:	

6.   What are the conclusions that can be drawn from the information we have learned about brain development?

a. _____

_____

b. _____

_____

c. _____

_____

d. _____

_____

e. _____

_____

f. _____

_____

g. _____

_____

h. _____

_____

Nature and Nurture

7.   Compare the roles of nature and nurture using the table below.

Nature	Nurture

How Does Motor Development Occur?

8.   What are the basic principles that govern human motor development?

_____

_____

_____

_____

_____

_____

_____

_____

_____

_____

_____

_____

How Does Intellectual Development Occur?

9.   Explain the concepts of assimilation, accommodation, and adaptation as they relate to
      infant and toddler development.

      Assimilation: _____

      _____

      _____

      _____

      Accommodation: _____

      _____

      _____

      _____

      Adaptation: _____

      _____

      _____

      _____

10.   Review the discussion in your text and Figure 9.3; construct your own chart recording the
      major points in Piaget's stages of sensorimotor cognitive development.

Stages of Sensorimotor Cognitive Development

Stage	Age	Behavior
1.		
2.		
3.		
4.		
5.		
6.		

11. Define the following terms.

Object permanence: _____

_____

Symbolic representation: _____

_____

Symbolic play: _____

_____

12. Refer to Figure 9.5. Identify the characteristics of enriched environments for young children.

_____

_____

_____

_____

_____

_____

Language Development

13.   Discuss Noam Chomsky's theory of language development.

_____

_____

_____

_____

_____

_____

14.   Discuss Eric Lenneberg's theory about language acquisition.

_____

_____

_____

_____

_____

15.   Identify and discuss the two sensitive periods of language development described by
        Montessori:

        a. _____

        _____

b. _____

_____

16.   Discuss the role of the environment in language development.

_____

_____

_____

_____

_____

_____

17.   Define and discuss the term *baby signing*.

_____

_____

_____

_____

_____

_____

18. Children develop language in predictable sequences. Identify each of the following sequences in language acquisition.

Sequence of Language Development

Holophrasic Speech
Symbolic Representation
Vocabulary Development
Telegraphic Speech
Motherese or Parentese
Grammatical Morphemes
Negatives

19. Refer to Figure 9.7. What are some of the important guidelines that will help promote children's language development?

_____

_____

_____

_____

_____

_____

Psychosocial and Emotional Development

20. Explain Basic Trust vs. Basic Mistrust, including the characteristics, approximate age, and how basic trust develops.

_____

_____

_____

_____

21. Social relationships begin at birth and are evident in the daily interactions between infants, parents, and teachers. What are the social behaviors of infants?

_____

_____

_____

_____

22. Define the following terms.

Bonding: _____

_____

Attachment: _____

_____

Adult attachment behaviors are: _____

_____

Infant attachment behaviors include: _____

_____

23. Discuss the issue of multiple attachments.

_____

_____

_____

_____

24. Refer to Figure 9.8 and describe the behavioral characteristics of the following
     attachment classifications.

     Secure: _____

     _____

     Avoidant: _____

     _____

     Resistant: _____

     _____

     Disorganized: _____

     _____

25. What is the role of fathers and infant attachment?

_____

_____

_____

26. What is temperament?

_____

_____

27. What are the nine characteristics of temperament?

a. _____

b. _____

c. _____

d. _____

e. _____

f. _____

g. _____

h. _____

i. _____

28. There are three classes or general types of children based on the nine temperament characteristics. Complete the chart below.

Children's Temperament Types

Easy
Slow to warm up
Difficult

Infant and Toddler Mental Health

29. Emotions and mental health play a powerful role in influencing development, especially cognitive development and learning. What are some of the threats to children's mental health?

_____

_____

_____

_____

_____

What are some of the outcomes of the threats to children's mental health?

_____

_____

_____

_____

What can early childhood professionals do to help children and families protect the child's mental health?

_____

_____

_____

_____

_____

30. Summarize the four reasons for the growth of the infant/toddler mental health movement.

_____

_____

_____

_____

_____

_____

Quality Infant and Toddler Programs

31. NAEYC defines developmentally appropriate as having the following three dimensions:

a. _____

b. _____

c. _____

32. What are the unique characteristics and needs of children during the first three years of life?

_____

_____

_____

_____

_____

33. Curricula for infants and toddlers consist of all activities and experiences they are involved in while under the direction of professionals. Curriculum planning for infants and toddlers includes the following concepts:

_____

_____

_____

_____

_____

_____

_____

Providing Healthy Programs for Young Children

34.   What is Healthy Child Care America and what are its goals?

_____

_____

_____

_____

_____

IV.   <u>Making Connections</u>

Go the Zero to Three website. Review the site to learn about the information available for parents and professionals. Add this site to your Internet log. Go to the Administration for Children and Families site. Read about initiatives in your state. Select the state profile option and print your state's profile. What do you find surprising? Is your state addressing the need for infant and toddler care adequately?   Be prepared to discuss your findings in class.

Zero to Three
http://www.zerotothree.org

Administration for Children & Families
http://nccic.org/itcc/

Multiple Choice Questions Select the best answer.

1.   Brain and child development research has several implications for those who care for young children. Which of the following is <u>not</u> a key factor for early childhood professionals to know?
       Hint: See **"Young Brains: A Primer."**
       A.   Babies are born to learn.
       B.   Remediation is more beneficial than prevention and early intervention strategies.
       C.   What happens to babies early in life has a long-lasting influence on how children develop and learn.
       D.   Critical periods influence learning positively and negatively.

2.   Human motor development is governed by certain basic principles. Which of the following is <u>not</u> a basic principle of motor development?
       Hint: See **"How Does Motor Development Occur?"**
       A.   Maturation of the motor system proceeds from gross motor to fine motor.
       B.   Motor development is from cephalo to caudal, or from head to foot.
       C.   Motor development is from distal to the proximal, or from the extremities to the central part of the body.
       D.   Motor development plays a major role in social and behavioral expectations.

3.   Does nature or nurture play a larger role in development? The question is the center of never-ending debate. Which of the following statements best represents the current thinking of the role of nature and nurture in development?
       Hint: See **"Nature and Nurture."**
       A.   Nature is currently viewed as the most important in development.
       B.   Nurture is currently viewed as the most important in development.
       C.   Both are necessary for formal development, and the interaction between the two makes us individuals.
       D.   The nature versus nurture debate is no longer an issue since we have brain research.

4.   Sensorimotor intelligence consists of six distinct periods of development. Which of the following is <u>not</u> one of the six periods identified by Piaget?
       Hint: See **"Stages of Cognitive Development: Sensorimotor Intelligence."**
       A.   Coordination of primary circular reactions
       B.   Primary circular reactions
       C.   Secondary circular reactions
       D.   Representational intelligence

5. The ability to acquire language has a biological basis, but the content of the language is acquired from the environment. Which of the following is true about a child's language acquisition?
    Hint: **See "Theories of Language Acquisition."**
    A. Parents and other people are models for language.
    B. Optimal language development depends on interactions with the best possible language models.
    C. Development depends on talk between children and adults, and between children and children.
    D. All are true statements about language acquisition.

6. Toddlers are skilled at using single words to name objects, to let others know what they want, and to express emotions. Identify one-word phrases that, in essence, do the work of the whole sentence.
    Hint: **See "Sequence of Language Development."**
    A. Referential speech
    B. Holophrases
    C. Grammatical morphemes
    D. Telegraphic speech

7. Two significant developmental events occur at about age two. What are those two significant events?
    Hint: **See "Sequence of Language Development."**
    A. Symbolic representation of mental symbols
    B. Vocabulary development and motor development
    C. Symbolic representation and vocabulary development
    D. Walking and talking

8. The stage of Erik Erikson's Theory of Psychosocial Development that applies to infants and toddlers and occurs from birth to eighteen months is which of the following?
    Hint: **See "Psychosocial and Emotional Development."**
    A. Basic Trust vs. Basic Mistrust
    B. Autonomy vs. Shame and Doubt
    C. Initiative vs. Guilt
    D. Industry vs. Inferiority

9. NAEYC defines *developmentally appropriate* as having all of the following dimensions except which of the following?
    Hint: **See "Developmentally Appropriate Programs."**
    A. Knowledge about child development
    B. Knowledge of appropriate curriculum
    C. Knowledge about the strengths, interests, and needs of each individual child in the group
    D. Knowledge of the social and cultural contexts in which children live

10. Developmentally appropriate programs for children from birth to age three are distinctly different from all other types of programs. Which of the following is <u>not</u> a dimension of a developmentally appropriate program for infants?
   Hint: **See "Developmentally Appropriate Programs."**
   A. Infants and toddlers learn by trial and error, repetition, and imitation.
   B. Infants are totally dependent on adults to meet their needs.
   C. Changes take place far more rapidly in infancy than during any other period in life.
   D. Infants need a great deal of independent learning opportunities to construct their own meaning.

11. Early childhood professionals must get parents and other professionals to recognize that infants, as a group, are different from toddlers. Infants need programs, curricula, and environments specifically designed for them. Which of the following statements is <u>not</u> true about appropriate environments for infants?
   Hint: **See "Developmentally Appropriate Programs."**
   A. Infants need adults who can tolerate and allow for their emerging autonomy and independence.
   B. Infants need adults who can respond to their particular needs and developmental characteristics.
   C. Infants need especially nurturing professionals.
   D. Infants need stimulating interactions and conversations.

12. Temperament is a child's general style of behavior. There are three general classes of temperament. Which of the following is <u>not</u> one of these types of temperament?
   Hint: **See "Temperament and Personality Development."**
   A. Easy children
   B. Children who are slow to warm up
   C. Hyperactive children
   D. Difficult children

Discussion Questions

1. List and explain the three dimensions of developmentally appropriate, as defined by NAEYC. Give classroom examples of the application of each dimension.

2. Discuss the characteristics of attachment. As an early childhood professional, what will your role be in developing positive attachments with infants and toddlers as caregiver? What will you do to help families, including fathers, maintain healthy attachments with their infants and toddlers?

3. Discuss the interest in infant and toddler mental health. Identify some of the threats to children, outcomes for children, and responses and solutions by early childhood professionals as explained in your text.

CHAPTER 10

THE PRESCHOOL YEARS: GETTING READY FOR SCHOOL AND LIFE

I. **Chapter Objectives**

Learner outcomes

The learner will
- Explain how the history of preschool education has influenced contemporary practice
- Identify the characteristics of a preschooler's growth and development
- Describe how play promotes children's learning
- Describe the purposes of play in preschool programs
- Identify the ways that the preschool curriculum is changing

II. **Chapter Overview**

Why are the preschool years so important?

What are the characteristics of preschoolers' growth and development?

Why and how are preschools so popular?

What is the role of play in children's learning?

How and why is the preschool curriculum changing?

What are important issues affecting preschool programs?

III.   Chapter 10 Study Guide

Directions: As you read the chapter, answer the following questions. Use the guide to study the chapter information.

What Is Preschool?

1.   Define the term *preschool* as used in the text.

_____

_____

_____

Why Are Preschools Growing in Popularity?

2.   List some of the reasons for the current popularity of and demands for preschool programs for three- and four-year-olds.

_____

_____

_____

_____

_____

_____

3.   Preschools are promoted as ways to accomplish the following goals:

    a. _____

    b. _____

    c. _____

    d. _____

    e. _____

What Are Preschoolers Like?

4. Describe today's preschoolers. Explain how they are different from those of previous generations.

_____

_____

_____

_____

_____

_____

_____

5. Describe the physical and motor development of the preschool child.

Physical and Motor Development of the Preschool Child

Physical Development

Motor Development

6. Review José's and Gisselle's portraits in Portraits of Preschoolers. How are José and Gisselle alike? How are they different? What does this mean for your classroom?

    _____

    _____

    _____

    _____

    _____

7. The preschool child is in Piaget's preoperational stage of cognitive development. List the characteristics of the child in the preoperational stage:

    a. _____

    b. _____

    c. _____

    d. _____

    e. _____

8. List the ways early childhood professionals can promote children's learning during the preoperational stage of development:

    a. _____

    _____

    b. _____

    _____

    c. _____

    _____

    d. _____

    _____

e. _____

_____

f. _____

_____

9. Review language development as described in Chapter 9. Discuss what significant changes take place during the preschool years. What relationship does family income have on language development of preschool children?

_____

_____

_____

_____

_____

_____

School Readiness: Who Gets Ready for Whom?

10. School readiness has many interpretations and meanings relevant to the perspective of teacher, child, parent, and national or state officials. Refer to The Readiness Puzzle (Figure 10.2). Define *readiness* and what the implications are for early childhood professionals.

_____

_____

_____

_____

11. Explain the maturationist view of child development.

_____

_____

12. Several readiness skills are identified in your text. Provide a brief summary of those skills, highlighting their importance and relevance for the preschool child.

Readiness Skill	Summary of Skill
Language	
Independence	
Impulse Control	
Interpersonal Skills	
Experiential Background	
Physical and Mental/ Emotional Health	

13. Elaborate on the following dimensions of readiness:

Readiness is never ending.

_____

_____

All children are always ready for some kind of learning.

_____

_____

Schools and professionals should promote readiness for children.

_____

_____

Readiness is individualized.

_____

_____

Readiness is a function of culture.

_____

_____

Play and the Preschool Curriculum

14.　　Play is the process through which children learn. Use the chart below to identify early childhood educators who valued play. List their views on play.

Early Educators and Play

Early Educator	View of Play
Froebel	
Montessori	
Dewey	
Piaget	
Vygotsky	

15. Children learn many things through play. Play activities are essential for their development across all domains. Play enables children to do the following:

_____

_____

_____

_____

_____

16. Much of children's play occurs with or in the presence of other children. Social play occurs when children play with each other in groups. Using the chart below, describe Mildred Parten's types of social play.

Mildred Parten's Types of Social Play

Unoccupied play
Solitary play
Onlooker play
Parallel play
Associative play
Cooperative play

17. Piaget recognized the cognitive value of play. Describe each of Piaget's four stages of cognitive play in the chart below.

Piaget's Four Stages of Cognitive Play

Functional play	
Symbolic play	
Playing games with rules	
Constructive play	

18. In additional to social and cognitive play, other types of play for young children are popular. In the chart below describe these types of play.

Informal or free play	
Sociodramatic and fantasy play	
Outdoor play	
Rough-and-tumble play	

19. What is the role of the early childhood professional in promoting a quality play curriculum?

_____

_____

_____

_____

_____

_____

_____

_____

_____

_____

The New Preschool Curriculum: Standards and Goals

20.   What are standards and how do they impact preschool children?

_____

_____

_____

_____

21.   The Early Reading First Program supports preschools and early childhood education providers by funding what?

_____

_____

_____

_____

22.   How are *goals* different from standards and how are they related to the preschool curriculum?

_____

_____

_____

_____

_____

23.   Quality preschools set goals in several curricular areas. In the spaces provided, identify
       the goals in each content area.

       A.   Social and Interpersonal

             1. _____

             2. _____

             3. _____

             4. _____

       B.   Self-Help Skills and Intrapersonal

             1. _____

             2. _____

             3. _____

             4. _____

       C.   Approaches to Learning

             1. _____

             2. _____

             3. _____

             4. _____

             5. _____

             6. _____

             7. _____

             8. _____

D.   Learning to Learn

   1. _____

   2. _____

   3. _____

   4. _____

   5. _____

   6. _____

   7. _____

   8. _____

E.   Academics

   1. _____

   2. _____

   3. _____

   4. _____

   5. _____

   6. _____

F.   Language and Literacy

   1. _____

   2. _____

   3. _____

   4. _____

   5. _____

   6. _____

7. _____

8. _____

9. _____

10. _____

G. Character Education

    1. _____

    2. _____

    3. _____

    4. _____

    5. _____

    6. _____

    7. _____

H. Music and the Arts

    1. _____

    2. _____

    3. _____

    4. _____

    5. _____

    6. _____

    7. _____

I. Wellness and Healthy Living

    1. _____

    2. _____

    3. _____

    4. _____

    5. _____

J.   Independence

     1. _____

     2. _____

     3. _____

24.   What is a learning center? What are a few of the learning centers suggested in the text (Table 10.2)?

_____

_____

_____

_____

_____

_____

_____

25.   Describe the components of a typical preschool schedule.

Preschool Schedule

| Opening Activities |
| Group Meeting/Planning |
| Learning Centers |
| Bathroom/ Hand Washing |
| Snacks |
| Outdoor Activity/Play/Walking |
| Bathroom/Toileting |

Lunch	
Relaxation	
Nap Time	
Centers or Special Projects	
Group Time	

Preschool Quality Indicators

26.   Quality is a major goal for preschool programs. Review the quality indicators and summarize the six indicators you feel are most important.

_____

_____

_____

_____

_____

_____

_____

_____

_____

Helping Preschoolers Make Successful Transitions

27.   Young children face many transitions in their lives. The transition from preschool to kindergarten can be a critical experience for young children. As an early childhood professional, what is your role in ensuring a successful transition?

_____

_____

_____

_____

_____

_____

_____

Preschool Issues

28.   Discuss the following preschool issues:

Pushing Children

_____

_____

_____

Access to Quality Preschools

_____

_____

_____

Universal Preschool

_____

_____

_____

_____

Funding Preschool Programs

_____

_____

_____

_____

VI.   <u>**Making Connections**</u>

Explore the NAEYC web site.

NAEYC
http://www.naeyc.org

Locate the Early Years are Learning Years segment of the web site. Review the articles listed. Locate and download at least three articles that relate to the growth and development of preschoolers.

Multiple Choice Questions Select the best answer.

1.   Preschool programs are popular today. Which of the following does <u>not</u> help explain the current popularity of preschool programs?
        Hint: See **"Why Are Preschools So Popular?"**
        A.   Many parents are frustrated and dissatisfied with efforts to find quality and affordable care for their children.
        B.   More parents are in the work force than ever before.
        C.   Publicly supported and financed preschools are currently available for all parents who are interested in their children attending preschool.
        D.   Parents, researchers, and others believe intervention programs work best in the early years.

2.   *Preschools* are programs for
        Hint: See **"Why Are Preschools So Popular?'**
        A.   Three- to five-year-old children before they enter kindergarten.
        B.   Infants to three-year-old children.
        C.   Prekindergarten children.
        D.   Toddlers.

3.   Preschools today have changed. Which of the following is <u>no longer</u> a predominant purpose of the preschool?
        Hint: See **"Why Are Preschools So Popular?"**
        A.   To support and develop children's innate capacity for learning.
        B.   To deliver a full range of health, social, economic, and academic services to children and families.
        C.   To solve or find solutions for pressing social problems such as preventing dropouts and stopping substance abuse and violence.
        D.   To enhance the social-emotional development of children.

4.   Preschoolers are in the preoperational stage of intellectual development. Which of the following is <u>not</u> a characteristic of the preoperational stage?
        Hint: See **"Cognitive Development."**
        A.   Children are able to conserve.
        B.   Children grow in their ability to use symbols.
        C.   Children center on one thought or idea, often to the exclusion of other thoughts.
        D.   Children are egocentric.

5.   All children need important skills to be ready for learning and school. Which of the following skills is an important "readiness" skill?
        Hint: See **"School Readiness: Who Gets Ready for Whom?"**
        A.   Language
        B.   Experiential background
        C.   Impulse control
        D.   All of the above

6. Language is the most receptive readiness skill. Children need language skills for success in school and life. One important language skill is the ability to listen to the teacher and follow directions. This important language skill is referred to as what?
    Hint: See "School Readiness: Who Gets Ready for Whom?"
    A. Receptive language
    B. Symbolic language
    C. Expressive language
    D. Communicative language

7. Children engage in many kinds of play. All of the following are stages of children's social play as described by Mildred Parten except _____.
    Hint: See "Kinds of Play."
    A. Unoccupied play.
    B. Occupied play.
    C. Solitary play.
    D. Associative play.

8. Early childhood teachers are the key to promoting meaningful play that promotes learning. In order to support a quality play curriculum, early childhood teachers should not do which of the following?
    Hint: See "Teachers' Roles in Promoting Play."
    A. Teachers support play by allowing children to compromise, resolve conflicts, and learn who they are.
    B. Teachers allow social play because it provides a vehicle for developing literacy skills.
    C. Teachers help children learn impulse control as they play.
    D. Teachers are responsible for creating play scenes to encourage fantasy play.

9. According to Piaget, play is cognitive development. Piaget described four stages of play through which children progress as they develop. Which of the following is not one of his four stages of cognitive play?
    Hint: See "Cognitive Play."
    A. Functional play
    B. Informal or free play
    C. Symbolic play
    D. Playing games with rules

10. Many early educators recognized the importance of play in a child's cognitive development. Which of the following early educators did not include play in the education of young children?
    Hint: See "Play and the Preschool Curriculum."
    A. Friedrich Froebel
    B. Maria Montessori
    C. Martin Luther
    D. Jean Piaget

11. Proponents of spontaneous, informal free-play activities maintain that learning is best when it occurs in an environment that contains materials and people with whom children can interact. The interests of the children generally determine play and learning episodes. Which of the following is <u>not</u> a problem that may occur when using the free-play format?
Hint: **See "Kinds of Play."**
   A. Professionals may interpret free play to mean that children are free to do whatever they wish with whatever materials they want to use.
   B. Some professionals may not plan what children are to learn while playing with the materials.
   C. Professionals are active participants, sometimes observing and sometimes playing with or helping the children.
   D. Sometimes professionals do not hold children accountable for learning from free play.

12. Parents seek quality preschool programs. All of the following are indicators of good-quality preschools <u>except</u> which of the following?
Hint: **See "Preschool Quality Indicators."**
   A. Pleasant physical accommodations
   B. Appropriate adult-to-child ratio.
   C. Mealtimes are quiet and teachers supervise; there is no talking, just eating.
   D. Emphasis on literacy development.

Discussion Questions

1. Define the term *transition*. Identify ways the early childhood professional and parents can help preschool children make transitions easily and confidently.

2. Review the preschool issues presented in your text. Identify one that you feel requires the greatest attention and what potential benefits it will have for all children.

3. Discuss the No Child Left Behind Act, the creation of preschool standards, and the implications for early childhood professionals and preschool children.

CHAPTER 11

KINDERGARTEN EDUCATION: LEARNING ALL YOU NEED TO KNOW

I.   **Chapter Objectives**

Learner Outcomes

The learner will
- Describe the history of kindergarten education from Froebel to the present
- Identify appropriate goals and objectives for kindergarten programs
- Describe developmentally appropriate kindergarten curricula
- Examine the issues that confront kindergarten education today

II.   **Chapter Overview**

What is the history of kindergarten programs from Froebel to the present?

What are appropriate goals, objectives, and curriculum for kindergarten programs?

How has kindergarten changed during the last decade?

What issues confront kindergarten education today?

III. Chapter 11 Study Guide

Directions: As you read the chapter, answer the following questions. Use the guide to study the chapter information.

The History of Kindergarten Education

1. Froebel's educational concepts and kindergarten program were introduced to the United States in the nineteenth century. However, kindergarten has undergone a dramatic change since its origination. Identify some of the changes that have transformed the kindergarten.

   _____

   _____

   _____

   _____

   _____

   _____

What Are Kindergarten Children Like?

2. Kindergarten children are like other children in many ways. At the same time, they have characteristics that make them unique. What are some of the characteristics of a kindergartner?

   _____

   _____

   _____

   _____

   _____

3.	Review Lina's and Ganali's portraits in Portraits of Preschoolers. How are Lina and Ganali similar to and different from kindergarten children you are familiar with? How can children's differences become assets in the classroom?

_____

_____

_____

_____

Who Attends Kindergarten?

4.	Froebel's kindergarten was for children three to seven years of age. What is the trend for kindergarten attendance in the United States?

_____

_____

_____

_____

5.	Discuss the issues and concerns related to the full- or half-day kindergarten debate.

_____

_____

_____

_____

Readiness and Placement of Kindergarten Children

6.	What is the definition of the *escalated curriculum* and what are the implications for kindergarten children and early childhood professionals?

_____

_____

_____

7.   Discuss the following alternative kindergarten programs:

Alternative Kindergarten Programs

Developmental Kindergarten	Transitional Kindergarten	Mixed-Age/Multiage Grouping

8.   Looping occurs when a teacher spends two or more years with the same group of same-age children. List the advantages of looping.

_____

_____

_____

_____

_____

_____

_____

9. Retention tends to be a political issue for early childhood education. Discuss the benefits and limitations of retention.

_____

_____

_____

_____

_____

What Should Kindergarten Be Like?

10. The early childhood professional is responsible for creating learning environments that are developmentally appropriate for children. List the ideas that early childhood professionals can put in place for developmentally appropriate practice in kindergarten.

_____

_____

_____

_____

_____

_____

Literacy Education and Kindergarten Children

11.   Literacy is an important and highly debated topic in early childhood education today. Define *literacy* and discuss the reasons why it is such a hot topic in education circles today.

_____

_____

_____

_____

_____

_____

_____

12.   With pressure from the No Child Left Behind Act and the standards movement in education, many states have created curricular guidelines to support teachers and focus their instruction. Review the State Guidelines for Kindergarten Reading (Figure 11.3) and discuss similarities and differences among the four states listed and what elements are most surprising to you.

_____

_____

_____

_____

_____

_____

_____

_____

13. Emergent literacy involves a range of activities and behaviors related to written language, including those undertaken by very young children. Identify the basic beliefs about literacy and how young children learn.

_____

_____

_____

_____

_____

_____

_____

_____

_____

_____

_____

14.   Define the following terms used when discussing literacy instruction.

Alphabet knowledge: _____

_____

Alphabetic principle: _____

_____

Comprehension: _____

_____

Grapheme: _____

_____

Onset-rime: _____

_____

Orthographic awareness: _____

_____

Phoneme: _____

_____

Phonemic awareness: _____

_____

Phonics: _____

_____

Phonological awareness: _____

_____

Print awareness: _____

_____

15. Refer to Figure 11.2 in the text. What are the twelve components of a research-based program for beginning reading instruction?

Children have opportunities to _____

_____

Children have opportunities to _____

_____

Children have opportunities to _____

_____

Children have opportunities to _____

_____

Children have opportunities to _____

_____

Children have opportunities to _____

_____

Children have opportunities to _____

_____

Children have opportunities to _____

_____

Children have opportunities to _____

_____

Children have opportunities to _____

_____

Children have opportunities to _____

_____

Children have opportunities to _____

_____

16. Literacy and reading are certainly worthy educational goals. However, how to best promote literacy has always been a controversial topic. Summarize the listed approaches to literacy instruction in the chart below.

Popular Approaches to Reading Instruction

Whole Word
Phonics
Language Experience
Whole Language
Balanced

17. The early childhood professional is responsible for supporting the emerging reading of the young child. Refer to Figure 11.5, Suggestions for Motivating Children to Read. Evaluate the list and select four you will implement in your classroom. Justify your choices.

_____

_____

_____

_____

_____

_____

18. What is shared reading and how does it support early literacy acquisition?

_____

_____

_____

_____

_____

Kindergarten Children and Transitions

19. Identify six ways that parents and kindergarten professionals can help children make transitions easily and confidently:

a. _____

_____

b. _____

_____

c. _____

_____

d. _____

_____

e. _____

_____

f. _____

_____

Kindergarten Issues

20.   Discuss the following kindergarten issues.

Redshirting _____

_____

_____

_____

_____

High-stakes kindergarten testing _____

_____

_____

_____

_____

Kindergarten entrance age _____

_____

_____

_____

_____

The Future of Kindergarten

21.   The author cites three ideas related to the future of kindergarten. List the three cited in the text and add two additional ideas of your own:

a. _____

_____

_____

b. _____

_____

_____

c. _____

_____

_____

d. _____

_____

_____

e. _____

_____

_____

IV. Making Connections

The National Association for the Education of Young Children (NAEYC) and the International Reading Association (IRA) issued a joint position statement on Beginning Reading in 1998. This is an important document for early childhood professionals responsible for literacy instruction.

Learning to Read and Write
http://www.naeyc.org/about/positions/pdf/PSREAD98.PDF

Download and print "Learning to Read and Write: Developmentally Appropriate Practices for Young Children." Read the position statement. Use the chart below to compare direct skills instruction with the approach described in the position statement.

Be prepared to share the information in class.

Direct Instruction	Balanced Approach

V. Chapter 11 Self-Check

Multiple Choice Questions Select the best answer.

1. Kindergarten has changed dramatically since it was first introduced to the United States in the nineteenth century. Which of the following is <u>not</u> an indicator of change in kindergarten?
   Hint: **See "Kindergarten Education: Learning All You Need to Know."**
   A. Kindergarten programs are more challenging, and children are being asked to learn at higher levels.
   B. All fifty states are required to operate kindergarten programs, and children are required to attend.
   C. More kindergartens are full day.
   D. More public and private schools and for-profit agencies are providing kindergarten programs.

2. Kindergarten children are like other children in some ways, yet they have characteristics that make them unique individuals. All of the following are characteristics of kindergarten children except which of the following?
    Hint: See "Characteristics of Kindergartens"
    A.   Socially, kindergarten children prefer to work in cooperative groups.
    B.   Most kindergarten children are very confident and eager to accept responsibility.
    C.   Kindergarten children are in a period of rapid intellectual and language growth.
    D.   Kindergarten children are energetic.

3. The practice of a teacher spending two or more years with the same group of same-age children is called _____.
    Hint: See "Alternative Kindergarten Programs."
    A.   Retention
    B.   Transitional kindergarten
    C.   Looping
    D.   Mixed-age/multiage grouping

4. Mixed-age or multiage grouping provides an approach to meeting the individual and collective needs of children. Which of the following is not a benefit?
    Hint: See "Mixed Age/Multiage Grouping."
    A.   In a multiage classroom, children have a broader range of children to associate with than they would in a same-age classroom, giving them more opportunities for diverse social interactions.
    B.   A multiage classroom provides teachers an opportunity to grow professionally by changing their grade-level assignments every year.
    C.   Mixed-age groups have a feeling of community and a sense of belonging because they spend at least two years in the mixed-age group.
    D.   Mixed-age grouping provides materials and activities for a wider range of children's abilities and allows for a continuous progression of learning.

5. Literacy has replaced reading readiness as the main objective of many kindergarten and primary programs. *Literacy* means the ability to do what?
    Hint: See "Literacy Education and Kindergarten Children."
    A.   Read and write
    B.   Recognize letters and their phonetic sounds
    C.   Read, write, speak, and listen, with emphasis on reading and writing well
    D.   Read, write, and communicate verbally within the context of one's cultural and social setting

6. _____ is the ability to deal explicitly and segmentally with sound units smaller than the syllable.
    Hint: See "Reading/Literacy Terminology."
    A.   Alphabetic principle
    B.   Phonological awareness
    C.   Phonemic awareness
    D.   Orthographic awareness

7.   Emergent literacy involves a range of activities and behavior related to written language, including those undertaken by very young children who depend on the cooperation of others and/or on creative play to deal with the material. The concept of emergent literacy is based on all the following beliefs except:
      Hint: See "**Emergent Literacy.**"
      A.   Reading and writing involve cognitive and social abilities that children employ in the process of becoming literate.
      B.   Most children begin the process of learning to read and write as soon as they enter school.
      C.   Literacy is a social process that develops within a context where children respond to printed language and to other children and adults who are using printed language.
      D.   The cultural group in which children become literate influences how literacy develops and the form it takes.

8.   Literacy and reading are important national and educational goals for young children and for everyone. How best to promote literacy has always been a controversial topic. The approach to literacy and reading that follows the philosophy of progressive education and that is child-centered, links oral and written language, and maintains that literacy should be meaningful to children is called _____.
      Hint: See "**Approaches to Literacy and Reading in Young Children.**"
      A.   Sight word approach
      B.   Phonics approach
      C.   Whole language approach
      D.   Language experience approach

9.   A _____ to reading is an approach that includes whole language methods and phonics instruction, and meets the specific needs of individual children.
      Hint: See "**Approaches to Literacy and Reading in Young Children.**"
      A.   Combined approach
      B.   Balanced approach
      C.   Basal approach
      D.   Direct approach

10.   The transition from home to preschool to kindergarten positively or negatively influences children's attitudes toward learning. Which of the following statements regarding success in kindergarten is supported by the research reported in the text?
      Hint: See "**Kindergarten Children and Transitions.**"
      A.   Children whose parents expect them to do well in kindergarten and who have teachers with high expectations do better than children whose parents have low expectations for them.
      B.   Children with less preschool experience have fewer adjustments to make than those who have been in school from a very early age.
      C.   Developmentally appropriate classrooms and practices have no affect on a child's success and learning.
      D.   Rejected children have no more difficulty with school tasks than other children.

11. Developmental and readiness screening are now being used to determine if children have the cognitive and behavioral skills necessary for kindergarten success. Which of the following is <u>not</u> a true statement about readiness tests?
   Hint: **See "High-Stakes Kindergarten Testing."**
   A. Many tests lack validity, or they don't measure what they say they are measuring.
   B. There is a mismatch between what readiness tests measure and what kindergarten teachers say is important for school success.
   C. Many readiness tests measure things that require teaching, such as colors, letters, and shapes.
   D. Readiness tests are quality predictors of which children may be retained in kindergarten.

12. Which of the following topics is <u>not</u> an issue facing early childhood professionals regarding kindergarten education today?
   Hint: **See "Kindergarten Issues."**
   A. High-stakes kindergarten testing
   B. Redshirting
   C. Kindergarten entrance age
   D. All of the above are kindergarten education issues

Discussion Questions

1. What are the characteristics of kindergarten children?

2. A primary goal of kindergarten education is for children to learn how to read. Teachers must support and guide children to help them learn what is necessary to be successful in school and life. Discuss the implications of this goal for children, families, and early childhood professionals.

3. Discuss the controversy over appropriate literacy instruction for kindergarten children.

CHAPTER 12

THE PRIMARY GRADES: PREPARATION FOR LIFELONG SUCCESS

I.   <u>**Chapter Objectives**</u>

<u>**Learner outcomes**</u>

The learner will
- Identify the physical, cognitive, language, psychological, and moral developmental characteristics of primary grade children
- Describe how the political and social climate are contributing to changes in elementary education
- Explain how the primary grades are being restructured
- Explain how the curriculum of the early elementary grades is changing
- Identify contemporary issues involved in primary education

II.   <u>**Chapter Overview**</u>

What are the physical, cognitive, language, psychosocial, and moral developmental characteristics of children in grades one to three?

What are the political and social forces contributing to changes in grades one to three?

How are grades one to three being restructured?

How is the curriculum of the primary grades changing?

III.   Chapter 12 Study Guide

Directions: As you read the chapter, answer the following questions. Use the guide to study the chapter information.

Teaching in Grades One to Three

1.   The curriculum and instructional practices in grades one to three are changing. Summarize these changes and realities that are occurring in grades one to three.

Diversity _____

_____

_____

_____

Achievement _____

_____

_____

_____

Testing _____

_____

_____

_____

Standards _____

_____

_____

_____

Academics _____

_____

_____

_____

Obesity prevention _____

_____

_____

_____

Planning _____

_____

_____

_____

Professional development _____

_____

_____

_____

Parent involvement _____

_____

_____

_____

Collaboration _____

_____

_____

What Are Children in Grades One to Three Like?

2. Why are children of today different from their same-age peers of the past?

_____

_____

_____

_____

_____

_____

_____

3. Identify the unique characteristics of primary age children in each of the areas listed in the chart below.

Characteristics of Primary Age Children

Physical development
Motor development
Cognitive development

4. Describe the unique characteristics of cognitive development of typical children in the elementary grades, as identified by Piaget.

_____

_____

_____

_____

_____

_____

_____

5. Define and describe the two stages of moral thinking typical of children in the elementary grades, as identified by Piaget.

Heteronomy _____

_____

_____

_____

Autonomy _____

_____

_____

6. Lawrence Kohlberg developed a theory of moral development. What are the three levels of moral development?

a. _____

b. _____

c. _____

7. Discuss the preconventional level of moral development.

_____

_____

Stage 1, the punishment and obedience orientation _____

_____

_____

_____

_____

Stage 2, instrumental-relativist orientation _____

_____

_____

_____

_____

8. Piaget's and Kohlberg's theories of moral development have the following implications for classroom teachers.

_____

_____

_____

_____

_____

_____

9.   What is character education? What are some traits included in the character education
        curriculum?

        _____

        _____

        _____

        _____

Primary Education Today

10.   Explain why the educational spotlight is on the early primary grades.

        _____

        _____

        _____

        _____

        _____

11.   Increasing student achievement and how to accomplish goals are at the center of the
        standards movement. Policymakers and educators view standards, tests, and teaching
        alignment as viable and practical ways to help ensure student achievement. Define the
        following terms related to the standards movement.

        Alignment _____

        _____

        Curriculum alignment _____

        _____

        Curriculum frameworks _____

        _____

12. Discuss the relationship between standards and curriculum alignment. What impact has the relationship had on the instructional models in the early primary grades?

_____

_____

_____

_____

_____

_____

13. Thinking skills are now included in classroom instruction. Review Bloom's hierarchy of questioning (Table 12.2). List the levels and at least two clues for questions for each level.

Bloom's Taxonomy for Early Childhood Classrooms

Competence	Clues for Questions

14.   Define and discuss cooperative learning.

_____

_____

_____

_____

_____

_____

15.   List the characteristics of the balanced approach to literacy education.

_____

_____

_____

_____

_____

_____

_____

_____

_____

_____

_____

_____

Looking to the Future

16. According to the author, schools will be asked to prepare children for their places in the world of tomorrow. Students will need to be empowered with the skills they can use throughout life in all kinds of interpersonal and organizational settings. List the skills identified as necessary to empower students for the future.

_____

_____

_____

_____

_____

IV. **Making Connections**

Go to the Phi Delta Kappan web site listed below. Explore the articles online and locate an article that relates to primary grade education. Print the article. Evaluate the information in the article and compare what you learn with the information in the text. Write a brief reflection detailing what you learned from the article and the text. Be prepared to discuss in class.

Kappan Articles Online
http://www.pdkintl.org/kappan/khome/karticle.htm

Multiple Choice Questions Select the best answer.

1.	Children today are different than children of yesterday. Which of the following is a fact that helps explain the differences?
	Hint: **See "What Are Children in Grades One to Three Like?"**
	A.	Children today are "smarter" than children of previous generations.
	B.	Many children bring to school a vast background of experiences that contribute to their knowledge and ability to learn.
	C.	More children are "minority" children.
	D.	All of the above are facts.

2.	A nearly universal characteristic of early elementary children (ages six to eight) is which of the following?
	Hint: **See "Motor Development."**
	A.	They are in a state of almost constant physical activity.
	B.	Girls' motor skills during this period are more advanced than those of boys.
	C.	They are no longer eager to learn.
	D.	They prefer to work alone.

3.	A major difference between the thinking of the preschooler and the early elementary child is which of the following?
	Hint: **See "Cognitive Development."**
	A.	The thinking of the elementary-age child has become abstract, and concrete objects are no longer required.
	B.	The thinking of the elementary-age child is not reversible.
	C.	The thinking of the elementary-age child has become more logical although concrete objects are still necessary.
	D.	The thinking of the elementary-age child has become less logical.

4.	Which of the following statements best describes the behavior of a child in stage 2 of Kohlberg's preconventional stage of moral development?
	Hint: **See "Moral Development."**
	A.	The exchange of viewpoints with others helps determine what is good or bad.
	B.	Children operate within and respond to physical consequences of behavior.
	C.	Concepts of right and wrong are determined by judgments of adults.
	D.	Children's actions are motivated by satisfaction of needs.

5.	Piaget identified two stages of moral thinking for typical children in the early elementary grades. Which of the following represent his two stages?
	Hint: **See "Moral Development."**
	A.	Punishment and obedience orientation, and autonomy.
	B.	Heteronomy and autonomy.
	C.	Instrumental-relativist orientation and punishment and obedience orientation.
	D.	Heteronomy and relations of constraint.

6. The theories of Piaget and Kohlberg and other programs for promoting moral development and character education have which of the following implications for primary grades?
    Hint: **See "Moral Development."**
    A. Children must have opportunities to interact with peers, children of different age groups and cultures, and adults.
    B. Students must have opportunities to make decisions and discuss the results of their decision making.
    C. Classroom climate must support individual values.
    D. All of the above.

7. Character education is rapidly becoming a part of many early childhood programs. New character education programs do <u>not</u> include which of the following?
    Hint: **See "Character Education."**
    A. Self-control, cooperation, and fairness
    B. Reasoning, respect, and responsibility
    C. Purposefulness, perseverance, and friendship
    D. Tolerance, good citizenship, and self-respect

8. Developing plans and selecting instructional strategies with the intention of promoting learning characterize what teaching practice?
    Hint: **See "Teaching Practices."**
    A. Intentional teaching
    B. Direct teaching
    C. Experiential learning
    D. Guided instruction

9. The process of making sure that the content of the curriculum matches what the standards say students should know is known as what?
    Hint: **See "State Standards."**
    A. Curriculum frameworks
    B. Content alignment
    C. Curriculum standards
    D. Curriculum alignment

10. According to Bloom's taxonomy, _____ is the highest level of thinking.
    Hint: **See "Thinking Across the Curriculum."**
    A. Analysis
    B. Evaluation
    C. Synthesis
    D. Comprehension

11. The following clues describe the _____ level of Bloom's taxonomy: demonstrate, calculate, compete, illustrate, show, solve, examine, change, discover.
    Hint: **See "Thinking Across the Curriculum."**
    A. Knowledge
    B. Analysis
    C. Application
    D. Comprehension

12. Students will require skills they can use throughout life in all kinds of interpersonal organizational settings, skills that do <u>not</u> include which of the following?
    Hint: **See "Looking to the Future."**
    A. The ability to read and to communicate with others, orally and in writing.
    B. The ability to successfully demonstrate knowledge on standardized tests.
    C. The desire and ability to continue learning throughout life.
    D. The ability to work well with people of all races, cultures, and personalities.

Discussion Questions

1. What are the characteristics of the primary age child?

2. Some advocates of basic education consider thinking to be real basis of education. Discuss the trend to teach thinking across the curriculum, including Bloom's taxonomy.

3. Discuss the standards movement and how it relates to teaching and learning in the primary grades.

CHAPTER 13

TECHNOLOGY AND YOUNG CHILDREN: EDUCATION FOR
THE INFORMATION AGE

I.   Chapter Objectives

Learner outcomes

The learner will
- Define *technology*
- Explain technological literacy
- Explain the terms *equity* and *access* as they relate to technology
- Explain how technology is used with special populations of children
- Describe the integration of technology into the early childhood learning environment
- Explain how technology has changed parents' roles in their children's education

II.   Chapter Overview

What does technological literacy mean for you, young children, and families?

What challenges do young children face with access to technology and technological equity?

How can technology help special populations of children, such as those with disabilities and those with limited English proficiency?

How can you integrate technology in the early childhood learning environment?

How has technology changed parents' roles in their children's education?

III. Chapter 13 Study Guide

Directions: As you read the chapter, answer the following questions. Use the guide to study the chapter information.

The Computer Generation

1. Children today are technologically oriented. They are the "dot-com" generation. Explain why the author refers to children today as the "dot-com" generation.

   _____

   _____

   _____

   _____

   _____

2. Define *technology*.

   _____

   _____

   _____

3. Technology is growing in the public schools and the lives of children. List some of the facts that demonstrate this growth.

   _____

   _____

   _____

   _____

4. Technological literacy is the ability to understand, use, and apply technological devices to personal goals and to learning. Refer to the New Jersey Content Standards for Technology (Figure 13.2). Complete the chart below to identify what components exist for each standard. Refer to this chart as a sample for technology standards for young children.

New Jersey Content Standards for Technology

Content Standard	Standard Components
A. Basic Computer Skills and Tools	

B. Application of Productivity Tools
 	
  1. Social aspects
 	
  2. Information access and research
 	
  3. Problem solving and decision making	

Equity and Access to Technology

5. Discuss the issues of equity and access to technology. Refer to Figure 13.3, Table 13.1, and the Diversity Tie-In "The Internet Digital Divide."

    _____

    _____

    _____

    _____

    _____

    _____

6. Young children's involvement has the following implications for you as an early childhood educator:

    a. _____

    _____

b. _____

_____

c. _____

_____

7. Define *equity* as it relates to technology.

_____

_____

8. To meet the technology needs of all children, teachers can do the following.

_____

_____

_____

9. Early childhood professionals must select software that depicts children and adults with differing abilities, ages, and ethnic backgrounds. All classroom materials, including technology, must be nonstereotypic of gender, culture, and socioeconomic class. Identify key points you want to remember when evaluating software for your classroom.

_____

_____

_____

_____

_____

Technology and Special Childhood Populations

10.   Define *lapware*. Provide some examples of lapware.

_____

_____

_____

_____

_____

_____

11.   According to Public Law 100-407, the Technology-Related Assistance for Individuals with Disabilities Act of 1988, *assistive technology* is any device used to promote the learning of children with disabilities. Complete the chart below regarding the components of assistive technology.

Assistive Technology

Kinds of Assistive Technology	Importance of Assistive Technology	Uses of Assistive Technology	Examples of Assistive Technology

12. What are the criteria for judging the appropriateness of assistive technology?

a. _____

_____

_____

_____

b. _____

_____

_____

_____

c. _____

_____

_____

_____

Implementing Technology in Early Childhood Education Programs

13. As an early childhood professional, what are some of the techniques you can use to individualize technology instruction for all children?

_____

_____

_____

_____

_____

_____

14. Early childhood professionals can use computers and other technology to help children develop positive peer relationships, grow in their abilities of self-control, explore adult roles, and develop positive self-esteem.

_____

_____

_____

_____

_____

_____

_____

_____

_____

_____

15. Discuss the Drill versus Discovery debate.

_____

_____

_____

16. How can technology support and facilitate higher-order thinking?

_____

_____

_____

_____

Parents and Technology

17. How has technology increased parent participation? Give examples.

_____

_____

_____

_____

_____

18. Discuss how parents and government officials can and are monitoring children's use of the Internet.

_____

_____

_____

_____

_____

You and the Technological Future

19. According to the author, what will need to happen to bring technology to the classrooms and prepare children for the future?

_____

_____

_____

_____

_____

IV.   Making Connections

Technology is an important part of today's society. Young children of today must be technologically literate to be successful in the twenty-first century. Early childhood professionals must provide the support and instruction necessary for young children as they learn about technology.

Go to the NAEYC web site and download the complete NAEYC Position Statement on Technology and Young Children. Print the position statement. Study the statement and consider the information in the text. Be prepared to discuss the seven major points of the statement in class. Place a copy of the position statement in your professional files.

Technology and Young Children, Ages 3 through 8
http://www.naeyc.org/about/positions/PSTECH98.asp

V.   Chapter 13 Self-Check

Multiple Choice Questions Select the best answer.

1.   What is the term best used to describe the ability to understand, use, and apply technological devices to personal goals and to learning?
      Hint: **See "Technological Literacy."**
      A.   Technology
      B.   Assistive technology
      C.   Technological equity
      D.   Technological literacy

2.   Technological literacy has many dimensions. The dimensions of technological literacy include all of the following <u>except</u>:
      Hint: **See "Technological Literacy."**
      A.   Understanding the language of the technological world.
      B.   Using navigational strategies to access and find information.
      C.   Understanding that online information is valid and true.
      D.   Staying literate or up-to-date on technology.

3.   Early childhood professionals are attempting to select materials that are nonstereotypic of gender, culture, and socioeconomic class. According to your text, when selecting nonstereotypic materials, which of the following should be considered?
      Hint: **See "Equity in Technology."**
      A.   Software should be available in multiple languages.
      B.   Software should depict children and adults with varying abilities.
      C.   Software should be nonstereotypic of gender.
      D.   All of the above are acceptable guidelines.

4.　There is a fear that access to computers and other technology may in fact create another class of illiterates. Which of the following is <u>not</u> helpful in eliminating the issue of equity and access?
   Hint: **See "The Internet Digital Divide."**
   A.　Require all students to complete projects in class using technology.
   B.　Provide additional time after school.
   C.　Use scaffolding strategies such as having more technologically literate students team and work with those who need to develop technological skills.
   D.　Work with parents who have computers and Internet access to form technological support groups to help other families.

5.　The "digital divide" refers to the fact that certain student populations have limited access to computers and do not possess certain fundamental skills with technology. Which of the following is <u>not</u> a recommended strategy to help close this divide?
   Hint: **See "The Internet Digital Divide."**
   A.　Team technologically literate students with those who need to develop technology skills.
   B.　De-emphasize technology in the classroom so students who lack prior experience will not be at a disadvantage.
   C.　Develop family night programs to teach parents without Internet access how to use the web.
   D.　Allow students to use school computers after school.

6.　The term *equity* means that all children have the opportunity to become technologically literate. Which of the following actions does <u>not</u> promote equity in the classroom?
   Hint: **See "Equity in Technology."**
   A.　Review all software used in the classroom to ensure it is bias free.
   B.　Allow students to spend the same amount of time on a computer in the classroom.
   C.　Allow students to use the computers in the classroom.
   D.　Encourage students who have computers at home not to use the computer in the classroom, thus allowing other students more time to become technologically literate.

7.　Programs designed for children under five represent the fastest growing educational software market. Software designed to be used by the parent and child as the child is held by a parent is referred to as _____.
   Hint: **See "Technology and Infants, Toddlers, and Preschoolers."**
   A.　Toddlerware
   B.　Lapware
   C.　Smart boards
   D.　None of the above

8. Assistive technology is considered useful for young children if the technology is appropriate. According to your text, which of the following is <u>not</u> considered a guideline for appropriateness of assistive technology?
   ***Hint*: See "Ethical Issues and Assistive Technology."**
   A. Technology should respond to specific, clearly defined goals that result in enhanced skills for the child.
   B. Technology should be compatible with practical constraints such as available resources or amount of training required for family, child, and teacher.
   C. Technology should promote peer interaction and support inclusive placements.
   D. Technology should result in desirable and sufficient outcomes.

9. Three challenges confront early childhood teachers in implementing an effective program of computer instruction. Which of the following is <u>not</u> one of the challenges?
   ***Hint*: See "Implementing Technology in Early Childhood Education Programs."**
   A. Their own personal acceptance of computers.
   B. Decisions about how to teach computer terminology to young children.
   C. Assurance that computers have a positive influence on children.
   D. Decisions about how to use computers in early childhood programs and classrooms.

10. Technology should be fully integrated into the early childhood curriculum. A fully integrated program includes all of the following <u>except</u>:
    ***Hint*: See "Deciding How to Use Computers in Your Program."**
    A. Making sure that there is a computer/technology unit for the classroom.
    B. Technology should meet the individual needs of all children in the classroom.
    C. Technology content should be integrated into the other curricular areas.
    D. Technology should not be used as a reward system for children when they complete their other tasks.

11. In 1988, Congress passed the Children's Online Privacy Act, which was designed to accomplish which of the following?
    ***Hint*: See "Supervision of Children's Internet Use."**
    A. Ensure the privacy rights of children and protect them from unscrupulous individuals and firms.
    B. Require web site operators to block inappropriate material from children's access.
    C. Provide all homes with *Cyber Sentinel*.
    D. Require all parents to monitor their child's use of the Internet.

12. Young children of today will need technology skills to be successful in the future. In order to ensure that children today will receive the technology they need for future success, early childhood professionals will need to commit to all of the following except: *Hint*: **See "You and The Technological Future and You."**
    A. Learn to use technology and gain the training necessary to be computer literate.
    B. Dedicate themselves to the developmentally appropriate use of technology and software.
    C. Recognize that technology and all its applications are not just add-ons to the curriculum, activities to do only when there is time, or rewards for good behavior.
    D. Understand young children come prepared to use technology and do not need guidance or extensive supervision.

Discussion Questions

1. Discuss the issues of equity and access to technology.

2. Discuss the benefits of assistive technology for all children.

3. Discuss the drill versus discovery controversy over software for early childhood programs.

CHAPTER 14

GUIDING CHILDREN: HELPING CHILDREN BECOME RESPONSIBLE

I. ## Chapter Objectives

Learner outcomes

The learner will
- Define *behavior guidance*
- Analyze the goals of behavior guidance
- Identify the essential components of effective guidance in early childhood programs
- Develop a philosophy for guiding children's behavior
- Analyze theories for guiding children's behavior
- Evaluate the issues and trends in children's behavior guidance

II. ## Chapter Overview

Why is it important to help children guide their behavior?

What theories of guiding children's behavior can you apply to your teaching?

What are important elements in helping children guide their behavior?

Why is it important to develop a philosophy of guiding children's behavior?

What are important trends and issues in guiding children's behavior?

III. Chapter 14 Study Guide

Directions: As you read the chapter, answer the following questions. Use the guide to study the chapter information.

The Importance of Guiding Children's Behavior

1. List the reasons early childhood professionals need to know about guiding children's behavior:

    a. _____

    _____

    _____

    b. _____

    _____

    _____

    c. _____

    _____

    _____

    d. _____

    _____

    _____

2. What does the term *behavior guidance* mean?

    _____

    _____

    _____

    _____

3. What are the teacher and parent behaviors essential for promoting self-regulation in children?

_____

_____

_____

Using Theories to Guide Children

4. What is the social constructivist approach to learning and behavior?

_____

_____

_____

_____

5. Define the following terms.

    Zone of proximal development: _____

    _____

    _____

    Adult/child discourse: _____

    _____

    _____

    Self discourse: _____

    _____

    _____

6. Explain how teachers and parents can guide behavior in the zone of proximal development.

_____

_____

_____

_____

_____

_____

7. How can teachers use scaffolding to guide children's behavior?

_____

_____

_____

_____

_____

8. Give an example of adult/child discourse used to guide children's behavior.

_____

_____

_____

_____

_____

9. What is the role of private speech in self-regulation of behavior?

_____

_____

_____

10. Identify the three Vygotsky/constructivist strategies teachers can use to guide children's behavior.

_____

_____

_____

Teacher Effectiveness Training

11. Thomas Gordon developed a child guidance program based on teacher-student relationships. Teacher Effectiveness Training (TET) uses communication as the primary means of helping parents and teachers build positive teacher-child relationships that foster self-direction, self-responsibility, self-determination, self-control, and self-evaluation. Describe the components of the TET model using the chart below.

Teacher Effectiveness Training

Problem Ownership	Active Listening	I Messages

Guiding Behavior: What Does It Involve?

12.   The goal of most early childhood professionals is to have children behave in socially acceptable and appropriate ways that contribute to and promote living in a democratic society. Effective guidance of children's behavior consists of the following nine essential elements:

a. _____

b. _____

c. _____

d. _____

e. _____

f. _____

g. _____

h. _____

i. _____

13.   What are your basic beliefs about discipline and behavior?

_____

_____

_____

_____

_____

_____

_____

_____

14. Part of knowing children and child development is understanding and meeting their needs. Maslow's hierarchy of needs identifies five basic needs that motivate behaviors. Explain each of the stages listed below and discuss their importance to guiding children's behavior.

Physical needs _____

_____

_____

Safety and security _____

_____

_____

Belonging and affection _____

_____

_____

Self-esteem _____

_____

_____

Self-actualization _____

_____

_____

15. Helping children build new behaviors creates a sense of responsibility and self-confidence. To empower children to take responsibility for their own behavior, an adult can do the following.

Give children responsibilities _____

_____

_____

_____

Give children choices _____

_____

_____

_____

Support children _____

_____

_____

_____

16. Early childhood professionals need to set appropriate expectations for children. Expectations are the guideposts children use in learning to direct their own behavior. Explain the following ways of setting expectations.

Set limits _____

_____

_____

_____

Classroom rules_____

_____

_____

_____

17. Setting limits is important for the following three reasons:

_____

_____

_____

18. Environment plays a key role in children's learning and their ability to guide their own behavior. Provide some examples for each topic shown in the chart below that will help you create a classroom that supports children's guidance of their own behavior.

The Supportive Classroom:
An Encouraging Environment:
Time and Transitions:
Routines:

19. Children see and remember how other people act; therefore, it is important for the early childhood professional to model appropriate behaviors. You can demonstrate the following techniques to help children learn through modeling.

Show _____

_____

_____

Demonstrate _____

_____

_____

Model _____

_____

_____

Supervise _____

_____

_____

20. The text notes that ignoring children's behavior is one of the most overlooked strategies for managing an effective learning setting and guiding children's behavior. Explain why this strategy is not used more frequently.

_____

_____

_____

When ignoring children's behavior, what other components of effective guidance must be present?

_____

_____

_____

_____

21.   Discuss the importance of developing a partnership with parents, families, and others.

_____

_____

_____

_____

_____

_____

22.   Everyone involved in the process of education has basic rights that need to be recognized and honored. Identify some of the basic rights of each group below.

Children's Rights	Teachers' Rights	Parents' Rights

23.   Explain how the early childhood professional can promote prosocial skills in the classroom:

a. _____

_____

b. _____

_____

c. _____

_____

d. _____

_____

e. _____

_____

f. _____

_____

g. _____

_____

h. _____

_____

i. _____

_____

24.   What is empathy? Explain the following guidance skills that will promote the
        development of empathy.

        Empathy is _____

        _____

        Model resolutions _____

        _____

        _____

        Do something else _____

        _____

        _____

        Take turns _____

        _____

        _____

Share _____

_____

_____

Development of Autonomous Behavior

25. What is autonomy and how is it achieved?

_____

_____

_____

_____

_____

26. What are "sanctions by reciprocity"? Give examples.

_____

_____

_____

_____

Physical Punishment

27. Is it possible to guide children's behavior without physical punishment? Discuss the controversy over physical punishment.

_____

_____

_____

28. Spanking and physical punishment are considered inappropriate forms of guidance. Identify the problems associated with spanking and other forms of physical punishment.

_____

_____

_____

_____

_____

_____

_____

_____

Trends in Guiding Children

29. Review the trends for guiding children. Identify one that you feel will be the most successful technique and one you will employ in your own guidance of young children.

_____

_____

_____

_____

_____

_____

_____

_____

IV.   **Making Connections**

Go to the Internet and use the search tool listed below. Search for more information on positive guidance strategies for young children. Print an article for your files. Be prepared to discuss your information in class.

Ask.com
http://www.ask.com

V.   **Chapter 14 Self-Check**

Multiple Choice Questions Select the best answer.

1.   Guiding children's behavior is best described as which of the following?
       Hint: **See "The Importance of Guiding Children's Behavior."**
       A.   A process of helping children become compliant to adult rules.
       B.   A process of helping children learn to submit to the control of authority figures.
       C.   A process of helping children learn to follow the rules.
       D.   A process of helping children build positive behaviors.

2.   Piaget and Vygotsky are associated with which of the following theories of child guidance?
       Hint: **See "A Social Constructivist Approach to Guiding Children."**
       A.   Self-regulation
       B.   Social constructivist
       C.   Hierarchy of needs
       D.   Adult/child discourse

3.   The range of tasks that is too difficult for children to learn by themselves, but can be learned with guidance and assistance from more competent others, describes _____.
       Hint: **See "A Social Constructivist Approach to Guiding Children."**
       A.   Adult/child discourse
       B.   Self-discourse
       C.   Zone of proximal development
       D.   Self-regulation

4.   Private speech plays an important role in problem solving and self-regulation of behavior. Children learn to transfer problem-solving knowledge and responsibility from adults to themselves. Which of the following does not support this transfer of learning?
       Hint: **See "Private Speech and Self-Guided Behavior."**
       A.   Adults direct children to use "I messages."
       B.   Adults use questions and strategies to guide children to help them discover solutions.
       C.   The use of language by adults leads children to use speech to solve problems.
       D.   The relationship of private speech to children's behavior is consistent with the assumption that self-guiding utterances help bring actions under the control of thought.

5.   Teacher Effectiveness Training (TET) is a child guidance program based on teacher-student relationships. Which of the following is <u>not</u> one of the cornerstones of the TET approach?
      Hint: **See "Teacher Effectiveness Training."**
      A.   Problem ownership
      B.   Active listening
      C.   I messages
      D.   Scaffolding

6.   Self-actualization is our inherent tendency to reach our true potential. Which of the following are components of Maslow's hierarchy of needs?
      Hint: **See "Meet Children's Needs."**
      A.   Physical needs, safety and security, and self-esteem
      B.   Physical needs, cognitive needs, and self-esteem
      C.   Safety and security, belonging and affection, and self-motivation
      D.   Belonging and affection, cognitive needs, self-esteem

7.   Parents and early childhood professionals who are working to empower children to develop control over their own behaviors will:
      Hint: **See "Help Children Build New Behaviors."**
      A.   Give children responsibilities.
      B.   Give children choices and help them make decisions.
      C.   Support children in their efforts to be successful.
      D.   All of the above choices will empower children.

8.   Setting limits helps children understand what the classroom expectations are and helps define unacceptable behavior. Setting clear limits is important for all of the following reasons <u>except</u>:
      Hint: **See "Establish Appropriate Expectations."**
      A.   Limits provide children with security.
      B.   Limits help the early childhood professional clarify what is unacceptable behavior in their classroom.
      C.   Setting limits solves the problem of misbehaving children because they know what is acceptable behavior.
      D.   Setting limits helps children act with confidence because they know what behaviors are acceptable.

9.   When establishing classroom rules, the early childhood professional must avoid which of the following?
      Hint: **See "Develop Classroom Rules."**
      A.   Plan classroom rules the first day of class.
      B.   Create as many rules as necessary to operate a specific program.
      C.   Consider the age and maturity of the children.
      D.   Establish rules that are fair and reasonable.

10. Environment plays a key role in children's ability to guide their behavior. Which of the following is not a suggestion for modifying the environment?
Hint: See **"Arrange and Modify the Environment."**
   A. Create an attractive and aesthetically pleasing classroom or center.
   B. Arrange the setting to be conducive for the behaviors you want to teach.
   C. Establish idle time for release of stress during extended transition periods.
   D. Establish classroom routines from the beginning.

11. More and more, early childhood professionals agree that it is possible to guide children's behavior without physical punishment. Which of the following statements is not a problem associated with spanking and other forms of physical punishment?
Hint: See **"Physical Punishment."**
   A. Physical punishment is generally ineffective in building positive behavior.
   B. Physical punishment such as spanking is best used with early elementary children.
   C. Parents, caregivers, and teachers are children's sources of security, and use of physical punishment takes away from the sense of security that children must have to function confidently in their daily lives.
   D. If used, physical punishment such as spanking is best used for early elementary children.

12. There are several trends in early childhood education relating to the guidance of young children. Which of the following is not currently a trend?
Hint: See **"Trends in Guiding Children."**
   A. Parent training
   B. The use of character education as a means of promoting responsible behavior
   C. Teaching civility
   D. Early intervention

Discussion Questions

1. Identify and explain five essential elements of effective guidance of children's behavior in early childhood programs.

2. Explain how teachers can structure the environment to promote positive child behavior.

3. Define *autonomy*. Describe how early childhood professionals can create an environment for learning that supports the development of autonomous learners.

CHAPTER 15

MULTICULTURALISM: EDUCATION FOR LIVING IN A DIVERSE SOCIETY

I. **Chapter Objectives**

Learner outcomes

The learner will
- Define *multicultural education*
- Understand the language and terminology associated with multicultural education
- Discuss the implications of a multicultural society for schooling
- Compose a plan for infusing multicultural content in early childhood curriculum, programs, and activities
- Explain the contemporary issues relating to multiculturalism
- Identify strategies for educating young children for living in a diverse society

II. **Chapter Overview**

What is multicultural education?

What implications does a multicultural society have for your teaching?

How can you and other early childhood teachers infuse multicultural content into curriculum, programs, and activities?

What contemporary issues influence the teaching of multiculturalism?

How can you educate yourself and young children for living in a diverse society?

III.   Chapter 15 Study Guide

Directions: As you read the chapter, answer the following questions. Use the guide to study the chapter information.

Multicultural Awareness

1.   Describe the demographic changes that will alter teaching and learning in the early childhood classroom.

_____

_____

_____

_____

_____

_____

2.   Define *multicultural awareness*.

_____

_____

_____

_____

3.   Figure 15.1 presents multicultural terms and definitions. List any new vocabulary words and their definitions related to multicultural education that you wish to recall.

_____

_____

_____

_____

_____

_____

The Cultures of Our Children

4.   The population of young children in the United States reflects the population at large and represents a number of different cultures and ethnicities. What are some of the implications of this diverse population for early childhood professionals?

_____

_____

_____

_____

Multicultural Infusion

5.   Define *multicultural infusion* and identify the related guiding principles.

_____

_____

_____

_____

_____

6.   It is important to assess your own attitudes toward children and families and to determine your multicultural awareness level. Revisit the questions in "Assess Your Attitudes Toward Children" on text pages 429–430, summarize your current awareness level, and identify any areas that you may need to focus your attention and learning.

_____

_____

_____

_____

_____

_____

_____

7.   What are the guidelines and processes for fostering awareness?

a. _____

b. _____

c. _____

d. _____

e. _____

f. _____

g. _____

h. _____

i. _____

8.   Selecting appropriate instructional materials to support the infusion of multicultural education is another important step in meeting the needs of the diverse learners in the classroom. Explain how each strategy contributes to the infusion of multicultural education. Give examples.

Multicultural Literature

_____

_____

_____

_____

_____

_____

Themes

_____

_____

_____

_____

_____

_____

Multicultural Accomplishments

_____

_____

_____

_____

_____

9.   What is sexism? Why is it an issue for early childhood environments? Explain.

_____

_____

_____

_____

_____

How does Title IX of the Education Amendments of 1972 address the issue of sexism?

_____

_____

_____

10. Identify some of the ways early childhood professionals can promote a nonsexist environment.

_____

_____

_____

_____

_____

_____

_____

_____

_____

_____

11. Describe an antibias curriculum.

_____

_____

_____

_____

_____

_____

12. Discuss the importance of teaching children conflict resolution strategies.

_____

_____

_____

_____

_____

_____

13. Identify the steps in the "no-lose" method of conflict resolution. Review the list on text pages 437–438 to generate new examples of conflict resolution.

Conflict Resolution Strategies

Steps	Examples

14. What is a learning style and what elements does it consist of?

_____

_____

_____

_____

_____

_____

_____

_____

_____

15. There are many ways you can provide for children's learning styles while responding appropriately to diversity in your program. Listed below are some of the suggested modifications for the learning environment. Provide examples of modifications that you would consider or would definitely use in your own classroom.

Modifications	Examples
Noise Level	
Light	
Authority Figures Present	
Visual Preferences	
Tactile Preferences	
Kinesthetic Preferences	

16. Early childhood professionals will work with children and families from diverse cultural backgrounds. Although it is important not to generalize, there are important elements of each culture that the early childhood professional needs to know. Identify the key elements of the Hispanic culture discussed in the text and the implications for working with Hispanic children and their families.

_____

_____

_____

_____

_____

_____

_____

_____

_____

_____

17. Identify the guidelines for involving Hispanic parents in their child's education.

_____

_____

_____

_____

_____

_____

_____

_____

18. The Bilingual Education Act, Title VII of the Elementary and Secondary Education Act (ESEA), outlines the federal government's policy toward bilingual education. What is the policy, and how does this relate to the classroom practices of early childhood professionals?

_____

_____

_____

_____

_____

_____

_____

_____

19. Identify a few of the reasons for the interest in bilingual education.

_____

_____

_____

_____

_____

_____

20. Early childhood programs for students with limited English proficiency (LEP) can follow several patterns. Identify the key elements of the selected programs on the chart.

Selected Programs for Students with Limited English Proficiency

Structured immersion	ESL	Transitional bilingual	Maintenance bilingual

Trends in Multicultural Education

21. Identify the trends that will affect how you teach the diverse groups of children in early childhood classrooms today and in the future:

    a. _____

    _____

    _____

    b. _____

    _____

    _____

c. _____

_____

_____

d. _____

_____

_____

e. _____

_____

_____

IV. <u>Making Connections</u>

Go to the web sites listed below. Read the article. Print the article and one activity.
Complete the activity and reflect on how it will help when working with diverse
populations of learners. Place the article and the activity in your professional files.

Defining Multicultural Education
http://www.edchange.org/multicultural/initial.html

Multicultural Awareness Activities
http://www.edchange.org/multicultural/activityarch.html

V. Chapter 15 Self-Check

Multiple Choice Questions: Select the best answer.

1. Multicultural awareness includes all of the following <u>except</u> _____.
   Hint: **See "Multicultural Awareness."**
   A. Appreciation and understanding of peoples' cultures, socioeconomic status, and gender.
   B. Lessons focusing on certain cultures regardless of the cultures represented by the class.
   C. Understanding one's own culture.
   D. Lessons focusing on methods, procedures, and activities, not terms and concepts.

2. Multicultural infusion is making multiculturalism an explicit part of the curriculum and programs. Which of the following is <u>not</u> a practice that encourages multicultural infusion?
   Hint: **See "Multicultural Infusion."**
   A. Promote and use conflict resolution strategies
   B. Encourage cooperative learning
   C. Teach to children's learning styles
   D. All of the above promote multicultural infusion

3. To infuse sensitivity into a multicultural classroom, the early childhood professional must carefully consider and select appropriate instructional materials. Which of the following is <u>not</u> a suggestion to follow when selecting multicultural literature?
   Hint: **See "Select Appropriate Instructional Materials."**
   A. Literature should emphasize people's habits, customs, and general living and working behaviors.
   B. Appropriate literature for young children focuses on only one difference such as culture, gender, or ability level.
   C. Literature should provide an authentic language experience.
   D. Literature should be written by men and women from varied cultures and reflect various writing styles.

4. The legislation that prohibits discrimination based on gender is which of the following?
   Hint: **See "Avoid Sexism and Gender-Role Stereotyping."**
   A. Title IX of the Education Amendments of 1972
   B. Title VII of the Elementary and Secondary Education Act (ESEA)
   C. The Civil Rights Act of 1964
   D. The Individuals with Disabilities Education Act (IDEA)

5. Characteristics of an antibias curriculum do <u>not</u> include the following:
    Hint: **See "Implement an Antibias Curriculum and Activities."**
    A. Help children to learn to accept others regardless of race, gender, ethnicity, socioeconomic status, and disability.
    B. Children learn to construct a knowledgeable, confident self-identity.
    C. Children learn to speak for themselves and others under sensitive guidance.
    D. Instruction of culture should begin in kindergarten.

6. When teaching conflict resolution strategies to children, which of the following is <u>not</u> one of the steps in the "no-lose" method of conflict resolution?
    Hint: **See "Promote and Use Conflict-Resolution Strategies."**
    A. Identify and define the conflict in a nonaccusatory manner.
    B. Invite children to listen carefully as you fix the problem.
    C. Put the plan into action.
    D. Follow up to evaluate how well the solution worked.

7. Learning styles consist of all of the following <u>except</u>:
    Hint: **See "Teach to Children's Learning Styles and Intelligences."**
    A. Environmental
    B. Emotional
    C. Cultural
    D. Psychological

8. There are several ways the early childhood professional can adapt the learning environment for the learning styles of children. Which of the following will <u>not</u> help to modify the environment for different learning styles?
    Hint: **See "Teach to Children's Learning Styles and Intelligences."**
    A. Allow children excessive freedom to guide their play and work by having authority figures remain in the shadows.
    B. Adjust the noise level by providing earplugs or earphones.
    C. Use manipulative and three-dimensional materials.
    D. Provide frequent breaks.

9. When working with families from diverse backgrounds it is important to <u>avoid</u> which of the following?
    Hint: **See "Welcome Parent and Community Involvement."**
    A. Use a personal touch.
    B. Be persistent in maintaining involvement.
    C. Provide strong leadership and administrative support.
    D. Avoid staff development that only highlights one culture or ethnicity.

10. Bilingual education is defined as which of the following?
    Hint: **See "Bilingual Education Programs."**
    A. Education in two languages for the purpose of academic instruction.
    B. Suppressing the child's native language to learn the dominant language of the school.

C.   Teaching children a second language.

D.   Teaching children both the home language and the primary language.

11.   Which of the following is a true statement about the current interest in bilingual education?

Hint: See "Reasons for Interest in Bilingual Education."

A.   It is considered unpatriotic not to learn English.

B.   Some states have passed "English Only" laws.

C.   If a child has a disability and does not speak English, his achievement will be less than his/her English-speaking peer.

D.   None of the above statements are true.

12.   Multicultural education is changing due to current trends. Which of the following trends will affect multicultural curricula, programs, and practices in the early childhood classrooms of the future?

Hint: See "Trends in Multicultural Education."

A.   Multicultural curricula are becoming less pluralistic, with a focus on knowledge and information about just the dominant cultures.

B.   Multicultural activities and content are being included in curricula from the time children enter preschool programs.

C.   Multicultural education continues to be important only in classrooms that have diverse groups of children.

D.   Multicultural education is not an issue for early childhood education.

Discussion Questions

1.   Instructional materials used to support the infusion of multicultural education must be carefully selected. Explain how multicultural literature, themes, and personal accomplishments are used to enhance the multicultural materials in the classroom. Give examples of each.

2.   Many teachers, in the name of equality, state: "It doesn't matter what color we are—we are all people." Explain why this statement is harmful, and give examples of more appropriate ways to work with classroom diversity.

3.   Parents and teachers should provide children with less restrictive options in play and in other learning experiences and promote a more open framework in which gender roles can develop. Discuss how you would explain this process to parents and what the benefits are for their child.

CHAPTER 16

CHILDREN WITH SPECIAL NEEDS: APPROPRIATE EDUCATION FOR ALL

I.   **Chapter Objectives**

Learner outcomes

The learner will
- Identify the reasons for the current interest in children with diverse needs
- Explain the reasons for full inclusion of children in early childhood programs
- Evaluate the issues relating to teaching children with special needs
- Review programs for gifted children and identify how they meet the needs of young children
- Explain the role of the early childhood professional in identifying and reporting child abuse

II.   **Chapter Overview**

What are the reasons for the current interest in educating children with special needs?

What are the legal, political, educational, and social bases for mainstreaming and inclusion of children in early childhood programs?

What issues relate to teaching children with special needs?

How do programs for the gifted meet children's needs?

What is your role in identifying and reporting child abuse?

III.   Chapter 16 Study Guide

Directions: As you read the chapter, answer the following questions. Use the guide to study the chapter information.

Children with Disabilities

1.   One of the most important federal laws is P.L. 101-476, the Individuals with Disabilities Education Act (IDEA) of 1990, reauthorized in 2004. Discuss the purpose and intent of IDEA.

_____

_____

_____

_____

_____

_____

_____

2.   Define the seven principles established in IDEA for professionals to follow as they provide educational services to children with special needs.

Zero reject: _____

_____

_____

Nondiscriminatory evaluation: _____

_____

Multidisciplinary assessment: _____

_____

_____

Appropriate education (FAPE): _____

_____

_____

Least restrictive placement/environment (LRE): _____

_____

_____

Procedural due process: _____

_____

_____

Parental and student participation: _____

_____

_____

3. What are the disabilities covered under IDEA?

_____

_____

_____

_____

_____

_____

_____

4.   What is an IEP?

   _____

   _____

5.   What are the purposes of the IEP?

   a. _____

   _____

   b. _____

   _____

   c. _____

   _____

   d. _____

   _____

   e. _____

   _____

   f. _____

   _____

   g. _____

   _____

6.   Infants and toddlers receive early intervention services under IDEA. List the purposes of
   the funds for infants and toddlers.

   _____

   _____

   _____

   _____

7. What is an IFSP?

_____

_____

_____

_____

_____

_____

8. Identify the benefits of family-centered services to children.

_____

_____

_____

_____

_____

_____

_____

9. Define the following terms.

Adaptive education: _____

_____

_____

Natural environments: _____

_____

_____

Full inclusion: _____

_____

_____

Partial inclusion: _____

_____

_____

10.   Full inclusion is the subject of great national debate. Explain the reasons for the controversy.

_____

_____

_____

_____

_____

_____

_____

_____

11.   Identify some of the pros and cons of teaching in inclusive classrooms.

Pros of Teaching in the Inclusive Classroom	Cons of Teaching in the Inclusive Classroom

12. Define and explain the continuum of services.

_____

_____

_____

_____

_____

_____

_____

13. What are the benefits of a continuum of services for children in an inclusive classroom?

_____

_____

_____

_____

14. Identify the most restrictive and the least restrictive placement for children.

_____

_____

15. Define the following terms.

Consultation: _____

_____

Collaboration: _____

_____

Itinerant teacher: _____

_____

Resource teacher: _____

16.   Collaboration will enable you to work with many individuals who will commit to working together for the benefits of the child. Summarize the forms of collaboration in the chart provided below.

Collaboration Models

Collaboration with Colleagues	Collaboration with Parents	Collaboration with Paraprofessionals	Collaboration with Administrators

17.   Students with ADHD generally display cognitive delays and have difficulties with learning. What is ADHD and whom does it affect?

_____

_____

_____

_____

_____

_____

_____

What three areas are most troublesome for the child with ADHD?

_____

_____

_____

18. List at least six teaching strategies that will help you teach children with disabilities:

   a. _____

   b. _____

   c. _____

   d. _____

   e. _____

   f. _____

Gifted and Talented Children

19. What legislation was passed to specifically provide for gifted and talented children?

_____

_____

_____

_____

How is *gifted and talented* defined?

_____

_____

_____

_____

20.   General education professionals can provide for gifted children in their classrooms through enrichment and acceleration. Explain the terms *enrichment* and *acceleration*.

_____

_____

_____

_____

21.   What are some of the suggested methods for meeting the needs of gifted and talented children in the general education classroom?

_____

_____

_____

_____

_____

Abused/Neglected Children

22.   The extent to which children are abused is difficult to determine but is probably much greater than most people realize. Discuss the statistics and factors that contribute to child abuse.

_____

_____

_____

_____

_____

_____

23. Public Law 93-247, the Child Abuse Prevention and Treatment Act, provides the legal definition of child abuse. Define *child abuse*.

_____

_____

_____

_____

_____

24. Distinguish between physical abuse and emotional abuse.

_____

_____

_____

_____

25. As a teacher, you are a mandatory reporter of child abuse. Summarize the process for reporting child abuse.

_____

_____

_____

_____

_____

_____

26. Public Law 107-110, the McKinney-Vento Homeless Education Act of 2001, provides that children of homeless individuals and homeless youth are entitled to the same free, appropriate public preschool education as provided to other children. Discuss some of the other problems children who are homeless may encounter and to what extent these problems may impact their development.

_____

_____

_____

_____

IV.   Making Connections

Go to ERIC Clearinghouse on Disabilities and Gifted Education site listed below. Read "ADHD and Children Who Are Gifted." Print the article for your professional files. Be prepared to discuss the article in class.

ADHD and Children Who Are Gifted
http://www.ericec.org/digests/e522.html

V.   Chapter 16 Self-Check

Multiple Choice Questions Select the best answer.

1. IDEA provides federal money to state and local educational agencies to help educate students with disabling conditions in all of the following age groups <u>except</u>:
   Hint: **See "Children with Disabilities."**
   A.   Birth to age three
   B.   From age six to age eighteen
   C.   From age eighteen to age twenty-one
   D.   All of the above are federally funded

2. The _____ is one of the most important documents in the education of children with disabilities. It constitutes a contract between the school system and the child and his or her parents.
   Hint: **See "Individualized Education Programs and Family Service Plans."**
   A.   LRE
   B.   FAPE
   C.   IEP
   D.   LEP

3. The IFSP is:
   ***Hint*: See "Individualized Education Programs and Family Service Plans."**
   A. An individualized family service plan that specifies what services children and their families will receive
   B. An individualized family service plan that specifies the individual education plans of the child
   C. An initial family service plan that specifies what type of schooling the child will need when entering school
   D. An initial family school plan that specifies when the child should enter school based on the disabling condition of the child

4. Family-centered services are an important component of early childhood programming. Programs that utilize family-centered services report results in all of the following areas except:
   ***Hint*: See "Benefits of Family-Centered Services."**
   A. Helping families make the best choices for their children by providing comprehensive information about the resources in their communities.
   B. Accommodating the individual child, family, and community differences through collaborative approaches to services.
   C. De-emphasizing the family's role as decision maker and partner in the early intervention process.
   D. Valuing children and families for their unique capacities, experiences, and potential.

5. Inclusive classrooms offer many benefits for children. In an inclusive classroom, children demonstrate which of the following?
   ***Hint*: See "The Need for a Continuum of Services."**
   A. Increased acceptance and appreciation of diversity
   B. Better communication and social skills
   C. Greater development in moral and ethical principles
   D. All of the above are benefits to inclusive settings

6. Full inclusion is the subject of great national debate for which of the following reasons?
   ***Hint*: See "The Full Inclusion Debate."**
   A. Court decisions and state and federal laws mandate, support, and encourage full inclusion.
   B. Some people believe the cost of full inclusion outweighs the benefits.
   C. Some parents of children with disabling conditions prefer that their children attend separate programs.
   D. None of the above.

7.   The early childhood professional must plan how to create inclusive teaching environments. All of the following will help teach children with disabilities and create inclusive settings to enhance the education of all students except:
     Hint: **See "How to Teach in an Inclusive Classroom."**
     A.   Accentuating what children can do rather than what they cannot do
     B.   Using only standardized assessment so that the family will always know how the child stands in comparison to children without special needs
     C.   Using multisensory approaches to learning
     D.   Encouraging parents to volunteer at school

8.   ADHD students generally display cognitive delays and have difficulties in which of the following areas?
     Hint: **See "Attention Deficit Hyperactivity Disorder."**
     A.   Attention
     B.   Mental retardation
     C.   Impulse control
     D.   Attention and impulse control

9.   Which of the following is not a true statement about ADHD?
     Hint: **See "Attention Deficit Hyperactivity Disorder."**
     A.   ADHD is diagnosed more often in boys than girls.
     B.   ADHD occurs in about 20 percent of all students.
     C.   About half of the ADHD cases are diagnosed before age four.
     D.   ADHD is a type of learning disorder.

10. Gifted and talented children are not covered under IDEA's provisions, but Congress has passed other legislation to provide for the needs of these children. Which of the following is not considered an area of giftedness?
     Hint: **See "Gifted and Talented Children."**
     A.   Visual/performing arts
     B.   Logical-mathematical reasoning
     C.   Creative thinking
     D.   Leadership

11. Which of the following statements is not true about child abuse today?
     Hint: **See "Abused and Neglected Children."**
     A.   An estimated three million incidents of alleged child maltreatment were reported to Child Protective Services in 2000.
     B.   The attitude that children are property partly accounts for the history of abuse.
     C.   It is estimated that only one in every three cases of child abuse is reported.
     D.   Both abuse and neglect adversely affect children's growth and development.

12. Homelessness results in developmental delays and can produce high levels of distress. Homeless children observed in child care centers do <u>not</u> exhibit which of the following behaviors?
    Hint: **See "Homeless Children."**
    A.   Short attention spans
    B.   Aggression
    C.   Speech delays
    D.   ADHD tendencies

Discussion Questions

1. Discuss the seven principles established by IDEA for early childhood professionals to follow as they provide educational and other services to children with special needs.

2. Discuss the value and need for early childhood professionals to collaborate and consult with parents, administrators, colleagues, and paraprofessionals when educating a child with special needs.

3. Discuss gifted and talented education. Explain how the regular classroom teacher can meet the needs of children who are gifted and talented.

CHAPTER 17

PARENT, FAMILY, AND COMMUNITY INVOLVEMENT: COOPERATION AND COLLABORATION

I.   **Chapter Objectives**

Learner Objectives

The learner will
- Analyze changes in society and families and how that change influences children and early childhood programs
- Discover why parent, family, and community involvement are important in early childhood programs
- Determine why it is important to involve all parents and families represented in early childhood programs
- Describe how early childhood professionals and others can encourage and support programs for involving families and communities

II.   **Chapter Overview**

How do changes in society and families influence children and early childhood programs?

Why is parent, family, and community involvement important in early childhood programs?

What are the benefits of involving parents and families in early childhood programs?

How can you encourage and support programs for involving families and communities?

III. Chapter 17 Study Guide

Directions: As you read the chapter, answer the following questions. Use the guide to study the chapter information.

Changes in Schooling

1. Identify three ways schooling has changed in the United States:

   a. _____

   b. _____

   c. _____

Changes in Families

2. Family demographics are changing, including an increase in the incidence of grandparents assuming the parental role. Discuss how these changes impact the early childhood profession.

   _____

   _____

   _____

   _____

   _____

3. Early childhood professionals can provide support for families in a number of ways. Explain each of the following supports for families and give an example of each.

   Provide support services

   _____

   _____

   _____

Provide child care

_____

_____

_____

Avoid criticism

_____

_____

_____

Avoid being judgmental

_____

_____

_____

Arrange educational experiences

_____

_____

_____

Adjust programs

_____

_____

_____

Be sensitive

_____

_____

_____

Seek training

_____

_____

_____

Increase parent contacts

_____

_____

_____

Education as a Family Affair

4. Early childhood professionals recognize the need for family-centered teaching. List the reasons for the focus on family-centered teaching:

a. _____

_____

_____

_____

b. _____

_____

_____

_____

c. _____

_____

_____

_____

5.   Even Start is an example of family-centered teaching. Discuss the Even Start program and the inclusion of families in the learning process.

_____

_____

_____

_____

_____

_____

6.   Explain two-generation and intergenerational programs.

Two-generation _____

_____

_____

_____

Intergenerational _____

_____

_____

_____

7.   Identify and explain the AVANCE program.

_____

_____

_____

_____

Guidelines for Involving Parents and Families

8. List the guidelines for developing programs for parent and family involvement.

_____

_____

_____

_____

_____

_____

_____

_____

_____

_____

9. Use the chart below to describe the six types of parent/family involvement and give examples of activities for each type of involvement.

Six Types of Parent/Family Involvement

Type of Involvement	Activities
Parenting Knowledge and Skills	
Communicating Between Home and School	

Volunteering at School and in the Community	
Supporting Student Learning at Home	
Involvement in Decision Making and Advocacy	
Collaborating with the Community	

10.   Home visits help teachers demonstrate their interest in children and families. Home visits also help teachers better understand their students by seeing them in their home environment. List the key factors in facilitating successful home visits.

_____

_____

_____

_____

_____

11.   List the guidelines for parent and early childhood professional conferences.

_____

_____

_____

_____

_____

_____

12. Providing the conference is appropriate for the young child to attend, there are several benefits to having the child present. Summarize the benefits of child participation in conferences.

_____

_____

_____

_____

13. When face-to-face conferences are not possible, a telephone conference is an efficient alternative. What are specific tips to consider when holding a telephone conference?

_____

_____

_____

_____

14. Single-parent families may have special circumstances to consider when involving them in the program. Summarize the basic points to remember when involving single-parent families in school activities:

a. _____

b. _____

c. _____

d. _____

e. _____

15. Language-minority parents are individuals whose English proficiency is minimal and who lack a comprehensive knowledge of the norms and social systems in the United States. Discuss the issues related to involving language-minority parents in their child's education.

_____

_____

_____

_____

_____

_____

16. Identify the guidelines provided in the text by Janet González-Mena for culturally sensitive family involvement.

_____

_____

_____

_____

_____

_____

17. Teenage parents have unique and specific needs. The early childhood professional must be sensitive to their needs and encourage their involvement as well. Discuss your role in the following.

Support in their role as families _____

_____

_____

Support in their continuing development as adolescents and young adults _____

_____

_____

Help with completing their own education _____

_____

_____

18.   There are national organizations dedicated to family involvement in school. Review the organizations listed on page 515 in the text. Find out if there are any local chapters in your area. List below the names and contact person for any groups you find in your city or state.

_____

_____

_____

IV.   Making Connections

Explore at least three of the following web sites for parents:

http://parenting.ivillage.com/
http://www.earlychildhoodnews.com
http://www.familyeducation.com
http://www.parents.com

Search the web sites to find three articles that will help you become a partner with parents. Print the articles and begin a parent information file with information to assist you in working with parents.

Share the information with your class.

V.   Chapter 17 Self-Check

Multiple Choice Questions Select the best answer.

1.   Today parents families, and communities are as much a part of the educational process as are the students, teachers, and staff. Efforts to involve families and communities in the process of educating the nation's youth are at an all-time high. What is one primary reason for these efforts to involve parents?
      Hint: **See the introduction.**
      A.   Schools and other agencies are expected to involve and collaborate with parents and families in significant ways.
      B.   Educators now expect that parents will be involved in the education of their children both at home and at school.
      C.   Parent involvement may mean that while teachers work with parents to help children learn, they also have to teach parents how to work with their children.
      D.   There is overwhelming evidence that involving parents, families, and communities in the school increases student achievement and promotes positive educational outcomes.

2. Early childhood professionals can help parents with their changing roles in all of the following ways except:

   Hint: See **"Changes in Families."**
   A. Providing support services to help families link up with other agencies and groups
   B. Expressing constructive criticism when they are not spending enough time with their children
   C. Offering child care and seeking extended services for families that need additional child care
   D. Adjusting programs to meet the needs of the changing families

3. Family-centered teaching is a style of teaching that focuses on meeting the needs of students through the family unit. Which of the following statements is not true for the family-centered model?

   Hint: See **"Family-Centered Programs."**
   A. The family has the major responsibility for meeting the needs of the child.
   B. Family issues and problems must be addressed first.
   C. Intervention begins prior to birth by providing prenatal care for the expectant mother.
   D. Teachers can do many things concurrently to benefit both the child and the family.

4. Which of the following is not a true statement regarding grandparents as parents?

   Hint: See **"Grandparents as Parents."**
   A. More grandparents are raising their grandchildren than ever before in U.S. history.
   B. Many of the children living with their grandparents are "skipped generation children" meaning that neither of their parents is living with them.
   C. Reasons for the increase in the number of children living with grandparents include drug use, incarceration, and teenage pregnancy.
   D. Twenty percent of all children under age eighteen are living in homes maintained by grandparents.

5. There are six types of parent and family involvement. Which one of the following is not one of the types of family involvement?

   Hint: See **"Six Types of Parent/Family Involvement."**
   A. Parenting knowledge and skills
   B. Collaborating with the community
   C. Involvement in decision making and advocacy
   D. All of the above are components of family involvement

6. To help early childhood professionals involve all parents and families, your text suggests all of the following guidelines except:

   Hint: See **"Guidelines for Involving Parents and Families."**
   A. Support parents in their roles as the first teachers of their children.
   B. Support fathers in their roles as parents.
   C. Understand it is the responsibility of parents and families to locate services and support they may require independent of the program.
   D. Learn how families rear children and manage their families.

7. Conducting home visits is becoming more commonplace for many teachers. Which of the following is <u>not</u> a true statement regarding home visits?

   ***Hint*: See "Home Visits."**
   A. Home visits help teachers demonstrate their interest in students' families.
   B. Home visits demonstrate that the school and teacher both value parent involvement.
   C. Home visits build stronger relationships with parents but do not improve student attendance and achievement.
   D. Home visits help teachers to understand their students better by seeing them in their home environment.

8. Communication is important in the school and family involvement process. All of the following are true statements about telephone contacts with family <u>except</u>:

   ***Hint*: See "Telephone Contacts."**
   A. Telephone calls are an efficient way to contact families when it is impossible to arrange a face-to-face conference.
   B. It takes less time on the telephone to build rapport and trust.
   C. It is important to constantly clarify what you are talking about.
   D. Your telephone contact may be the major part of the family's support system.

9. When conducting successful parent conferences, the early childhood professional should do all of the following <u>except</u>:

   ***Hint*: See "Parent Conferences."**
   A. Plan ahead
   B. Portray an authoritative atmosphere
   C. Communicate at the parents' levels
   D. Develop an action plan

10. When involving single and working parents in school activities, the early childhood professional should consider which of the following guidelines?

    ***Hint*: See "Involving Single and Working Parents."**
    A. Sponsor evening and weekend learning activities at which parents can participate and learn with their children.
    B. Work with local businesses to arrange release time from work so that parents can attend conferences, volunteer, or in other ways spend time in their child's school when it is in session.
    C. Create a class web page the parents can frequently visit for updates about activities and their child's progress.
    D. All of the above are guidelines to follow when involving single and working parents in school activities.

11. Culturally sensitive family involvement is important for all the following reasons except:
Hint: **See "Language-Minority Parents and Families."**
   A. Language-minority families often lack information about the U.S. educational system.
   B. The U.S. educational system may be quite different from schools with which language-minority families are familiar.
   C. Language-minority families do not value education—they value work.
   D. The demographic makeup of the United States is rapidly changing.

12. Teenage families frequently live in extended families, and the child's grandmother serves as the primary caregiver. When working with teenage families, the early childhood professional should remember that teenage families have which of the following needs?
Hint: **See "Teenage Parents."**
   A. They need help with completing their own education because the education of the mother is a critical influence on the child's development.
   B. They need an authoritarian atmosphere because they are still children themselves.
   C. They need a plan of action because they do not know how to help their child.
   D. They need an opportunity to participate in fairs and bazaars to involve them in fund-raising activities of the school.

Discussion Questions

1. What are family-centered programs? Explain the benefits of such programs.

2. Identify three strategies for involving parents in their child's education and give the benefits of that particular strategy.

3. Parent-teacher conferences are critical for helping families and professionals accomplish their goals for the child. Discuss the guidelines for preparing and conducting successful parent conferences.

SELF-CHECK ANSWER KEY BY CHAPTER

<u>CHAPTER 1</u> **You and Early Childhood Education: What Does It Mean to Be a Professional?**

1.	B	9.	B	**Discussion**	
2.	B	10.	B	1.	See Chapter 1
3.	A	11.	C	2.	See pages 16–17
4.	D	12.	A	3.	See pages 11–16
5.	A				
6.	D				
7.	A				
8.	B				

<u>CHAPTER 2</u> **Early Childhood Education Today: Public Policy and Current Issues**

1.	D	9.	B	**Discussion**	
2.	B	10.	B	1.	See pages 32–34
3.	A	11.	D	2.	See pages 49–50
4.	A	12.	A	3.	See pages 50–51
5.	A				
6.	B				
7.	D				
8.	A				

<u>CHAPTER 3</u> **Observing and Assessing Young Children: Effective Teaching Through Appropriate Evaluation**

1.	C	9.	C	**Discussion**	
2.	A	10.	D	1.	See pages 64–71
3.	C	11.	A	2.	See pages 72–73
4.	B	12.	C	3.	See pages 60–61
5.	A				
6.	D				
7.	D				
8.	B				

<u>CHAPTER 4</u> **The Past and the Present: Prologue to the Future**

1.	A	9.	A	**Discussion**	
2.	A	10.	A	1.	See pages 85–86
3.	C	11.	B	2.	See pages 86–98
4.	D	12.	C	3.	See pages 104–106
5.	B				
6.	A				
7.	D				
8.	D				

CHAPTER 5 Theories Applied to Teaching and Learning: Foundations for Practice

1.	C	9.	B	**Discussion**	
2.	D	10.	A	1.	See pages 114–115
3.	D	11.	B	2.	See pages 128–130
4.	C	12.	D	3.	See pages 130–132
5.	B				
6.	C				
7.	D				
8.	B				

CHAPTER 6 Early Childhood Programs: Applying Theories to Practice

1.	C	9.	A	**Discussion**	
2.	D	10.	D	1.	See pages 140–147
3.	A	11.	D	2.	See pages 150–158
4.	B	12.	C	3.	See pages 158–163
5.	C				
6.	C				
7.	C				
8.	B				

CHAPTER 7 Child Care: Meeting the Needs of Children, Parents, and Families

1.	D	9.	C	**Discussion**	
2.	A	10.	D	1.	See pages 192–196
3.	B	11.	A	2.	See pages 179–189
4.	C	12.	B	3.	See page 191
5.	A				
6.	B				
7.	B				
8.	B				

CHAPTER 8 The Federal Government: Supporting Children's Success

1.	D	9.	A	**Discussion**	
2.	B	10.	D	1.	See pages 203–206
3.	C	11.	B	2.	See pages 203–208
4.	D	12.	C	3.	See page 212
5.	C				
6.	D				
7.	B				
8.	C				

CHAPTER 9 Infants and Toddlers: Foundation Years for Learning

1.	B	9.	B	**Discussion**	
2.	C	10.	D	1.	See pages 258–262
3.	C	11.	A	2.	See pages 253–256
4.	A	12.	C	3.	See pages 257–258
5.	D				
6.	B				
7.	C				
8.	A				

CHAPTER 10   The Preschool Years: Getting Ready for School and Life

					Discussion	
1.	C	9.	B			
2.	A	10.	C		1.	See pages 300–303
3.	D	11.	C		2.	See pages 303–304
4.	A	12.	C		3.	See pages 290–293
5.	D					
6.	A					
7.	B					
8.	D					

CHAPTER 11   Kindergarten Education: Learning All You Need to Know

					Discussion	
1.	B	9.	B			
2.	A	10.	A		1.	See pages 309–313
3.	C	11.	D		2.	See pages 319–325
4.	B	12.	D		3.	See pages 319–329
5.	C					
6.	C					
7.	B					
8.	D					

CHAPTER 12   The Primary Grades: Preparation for Lifelong Success

					Discussion	
1.	D	9.	D			
2.	A	10.	B		1.	See pages 343–349
3.	C	11.	C		2.	See pages 357–358
4.	D	12.	B		3.	See pages 352–356
5.	B					
6.	D					
7.	D					
8.	A					

CHAPTER 13   Technology and Young Children: Education for the Information Age

					Discussion	
1.	D	9.	B			
2.	C	10.	A		1.	See pages 373–374
3.	D	11.	A		2.	See pages 376–384
4.	A	12.	D		3.	See pages 385–388
5.	B					
6.	B					
7.	B					
8.	C					

CHAPTER 14   Guiding Children: Helping Children Become Responsible

					Discussion	
1.	D	9.	B			
2.	B	10.	C		1.	See pages 404–418
3.	C	11.	D		2.	See pages 411–414
4.	A	12.	B		3.	See pages 418–419
5.	D					
6.	A					
7.	D					
8.	C					

CHAPTER 15 **Multiculturalism: Education for Living in a Diverse Society**

1.	B	9.	D	**Discussion**	
2.	D	10.	A	1.	See pages 429–436
3.	B	11.	B	2.	See page 436
4.	A	12.	B	3.	See pages 434–436
5.	D				
6.	B				
7.	C				
8.	A				

CHAPTER 16 **Children with Special Needs: Appropriate Education for All**

1.	D	9.	D	**Discussion**	
2.	C	10.	B	1.	See pages 458–459
3.	A	11.	C	2.	See pages 471–478
4.	C	12.	D	3.	See pages 483–485
5.	D				
6.	A				
7.	B				
8.	D				

CHAPTER 17 **Parent, Family, and Community Involvement:**
Cooperation and Collaboration

1.	D	9.	B	**Discussion**	
2.	B	10.	D	1.	See pages 500–501
3.	C	11.	C	2.	See pages 502–507
4.	D	12.	A	3.	See pages 508–514
5.	D				
6.	C				
7.	C				
8.	B				